EARLY DAYS

THE BEST OF LED ZEPPELIN VOLUME ONE

© 2006 by Faber Music Ltd
First published in 2000 by International Music Publications Ltd
International Music Publications Ltd is a Faber Music company
3 Queen Square, London WC1N 3AU
Printed in England by Caligraving Ltd
All rights reserved

ISBN 0-571-52544-X

To buy Faber Music publications or to find out about the full range of titles available,
please contact your local music retailer or Faber Music sales enquiries:

Faber Music Ltd, Burnt Mill, Elizabeth Way, Harlow, CM20 2HX England
Tel: +44(0)1279 82 89 82   Fax: +44(0)1279 82 89 83
sales@fabermusic.com   fabermusic.com

GOOD TIMES, BAD TIMES

Words & Music by
Jimmy Page, John Paul Jones and John Bonham

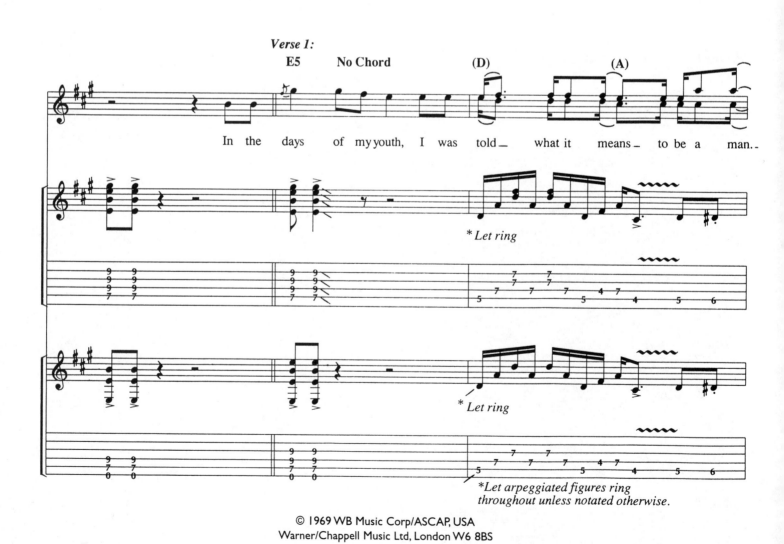

Key signature indicates E Mixolydian mode.

Verse 1:

In the days of my youth, I was told____ what it means____ to be a man...

*Let ring

*Let ring

*Let arpeggiated figures ring
throughout unless notated otherwise.*

And now I've reached that age — I've tried to do —

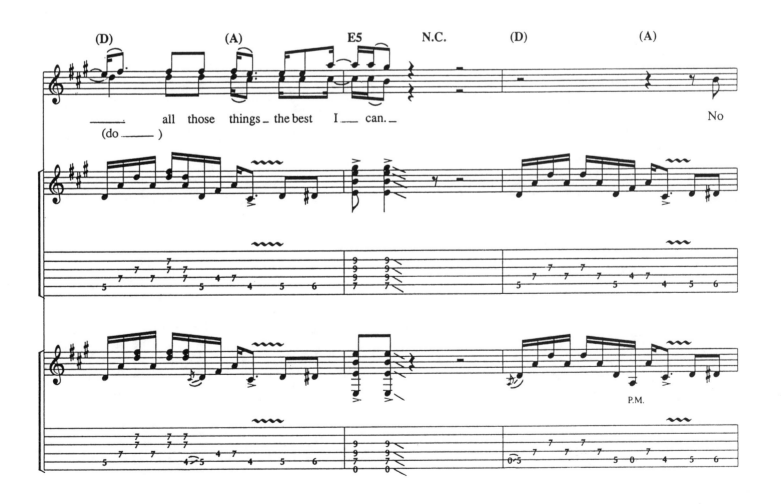

—. all those things — the best I — can. —

(do ——)

No

mat-ter how I try__ I find my way in-to the same__ old__ jam.__

Chorus:

Good times, bad__ times,__ you know I've had__ my share.__ Well, my

woman left home for a brown-eyed man,__ but I still don't seem to care.___

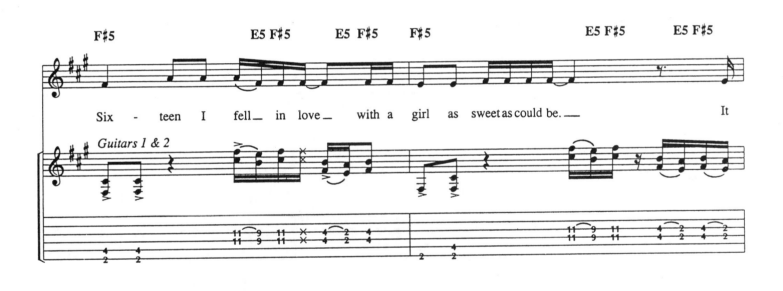

Six - teen I fell__ in love__ with a girl as sweet as could be.__ It

on - ly took a coup - le of days__ 'till she was rid of me.__ She

swore that she would be — all mine and love me 'till the end, — but

when I whis-pered in her ear — I lost an - oth- er friend. — Oh!

Parenthesised notes played by Guitar 1 only

Chorus:

Good times, bad times, — you know I've had my share. — Well, my

Electric Guitar 1

Electric Guitar 2

Let ring   *Let ring*

wo-man left home for a brown-eyed man,____ but I still don't seem to care. ____

(F♯sus4)

Guitar Solo
With Fill 1 (8 times)

Fill 1

Even gliss.

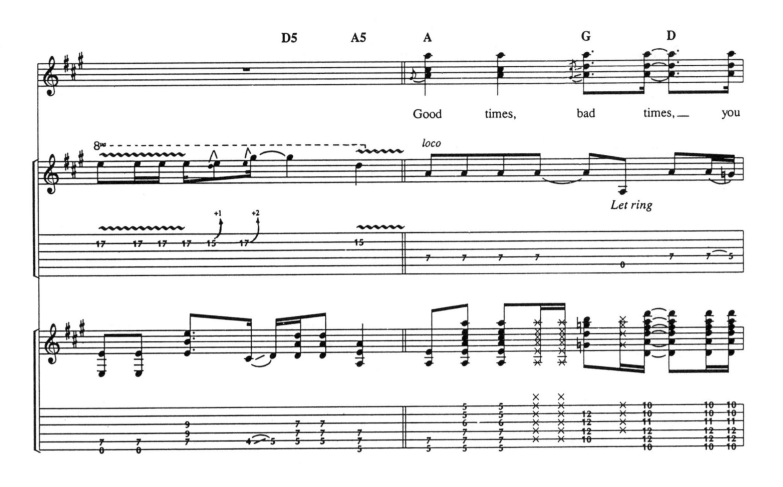

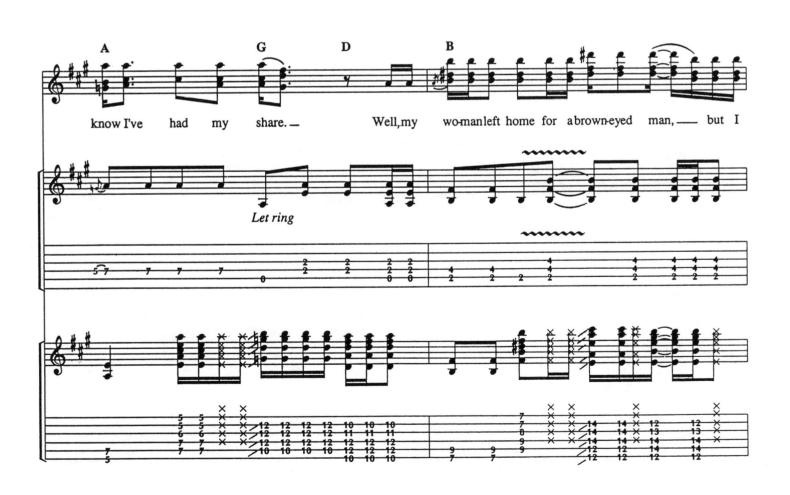

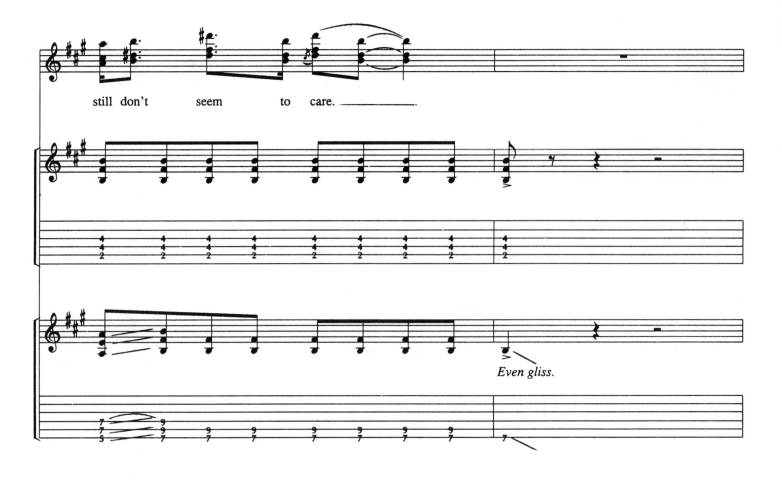

still don't seem to care. _____

Even gliss.

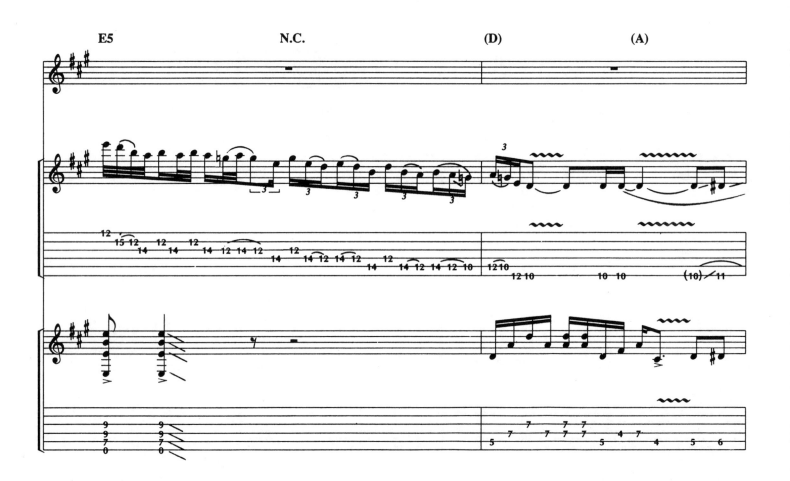

E5   N.C.   (D)   (A)

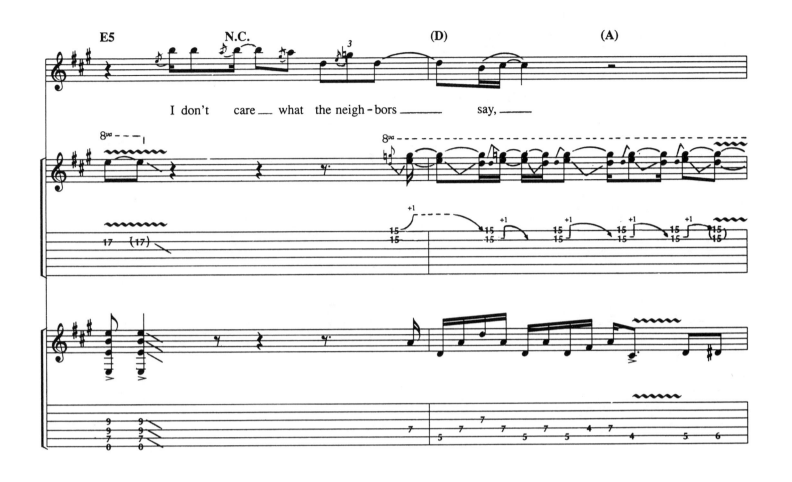

I don't care __ what the neigh-bors _____ say, ____

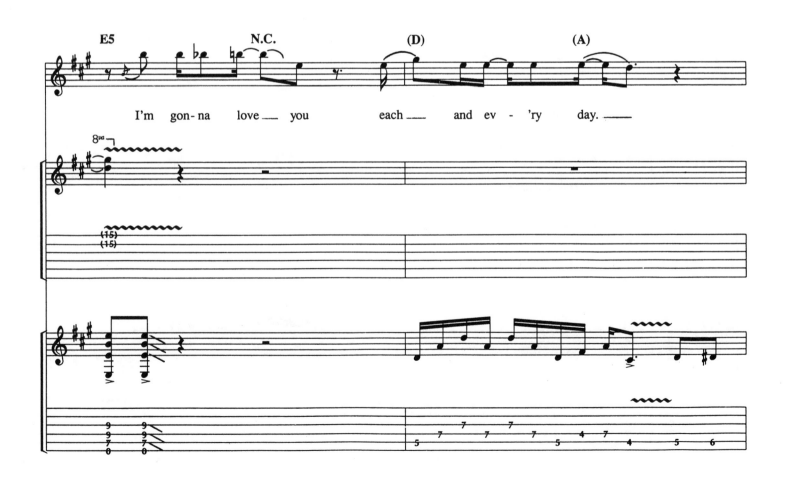

I'm gon-na love __ you each __ and ev - 'ry day. __

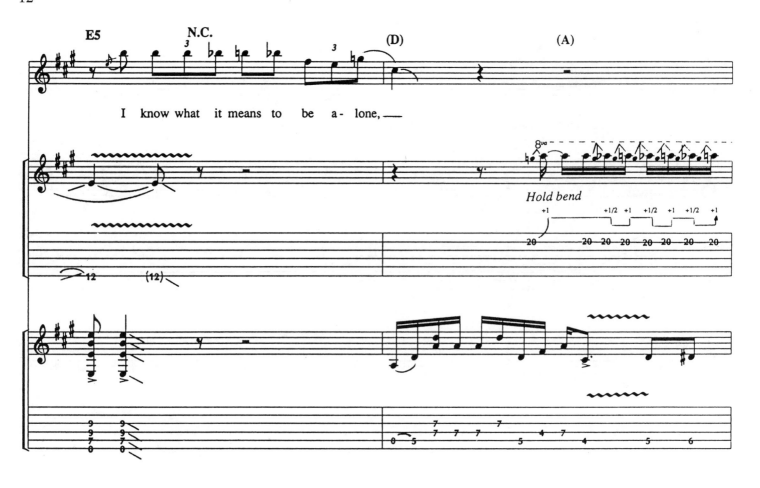

I know what it means to be a- lone,____

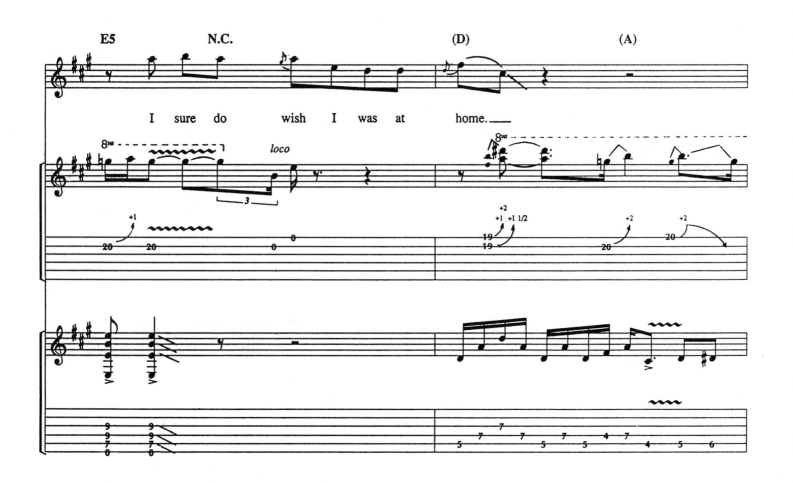

I sure do wish I was at home.____

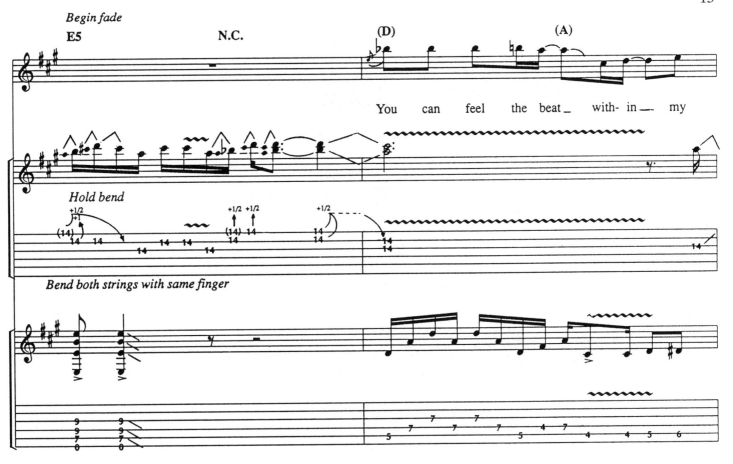

You can feel the beat _ with- in _ my

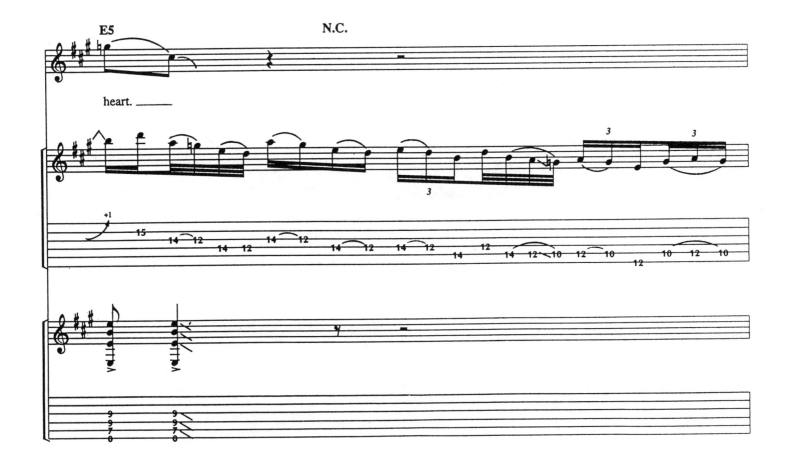

heart. _____

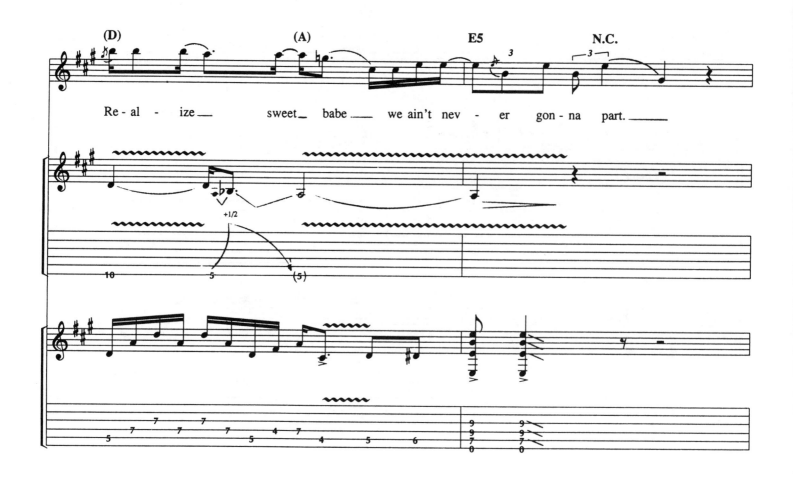

Re - al - ize____ sweet__ babe_____ we ain't nev - er gon - na part._____

Fade out

BABE I'M GONNA LEAVE YOU

Words & Music by
Anne Bredon, Jimmy Page and Robert Plant

Moderately slow with halftime feel ♩ = 138
Intro:

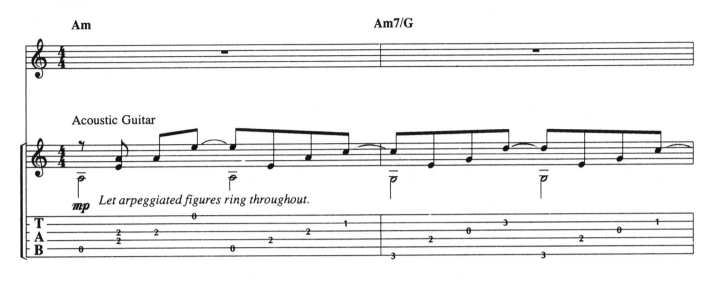

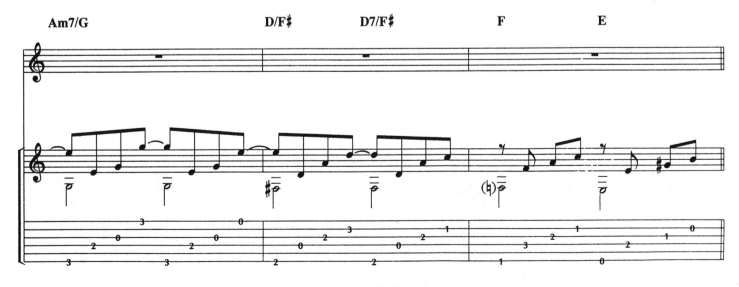

16

Verse 1:

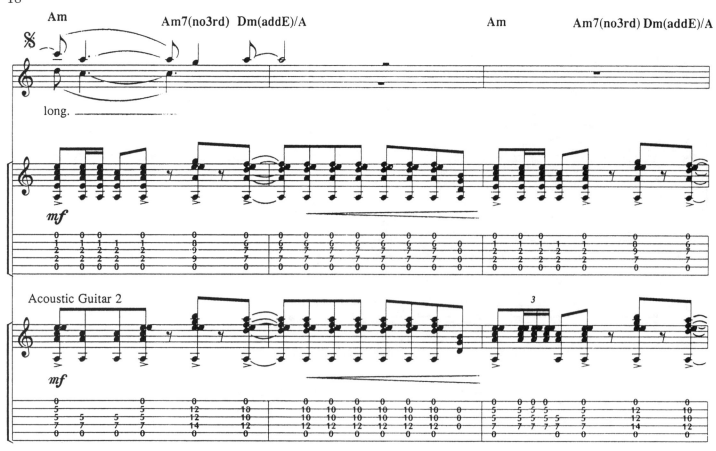

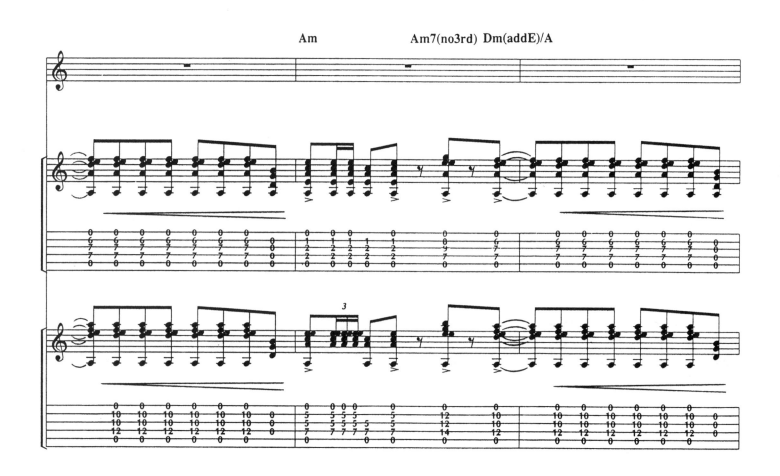

Coda 1

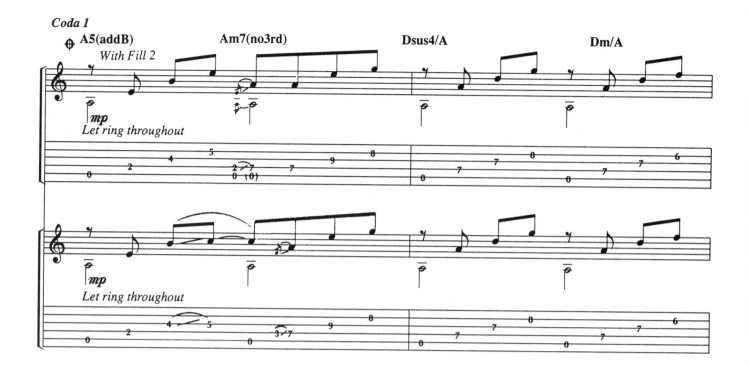

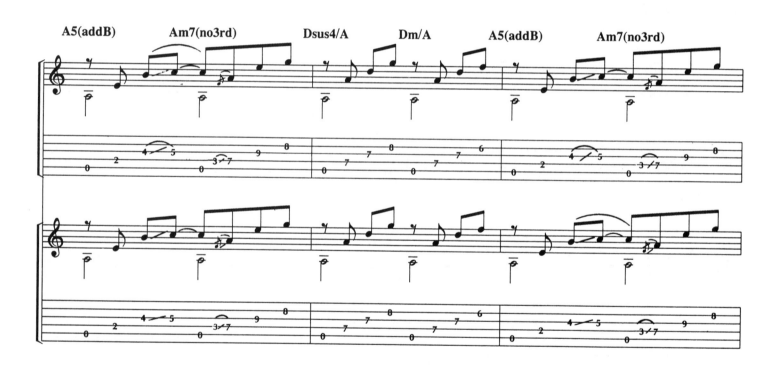

Fill 2

Slide Guitar *(with backwards echo)*

Tuning: ① =D

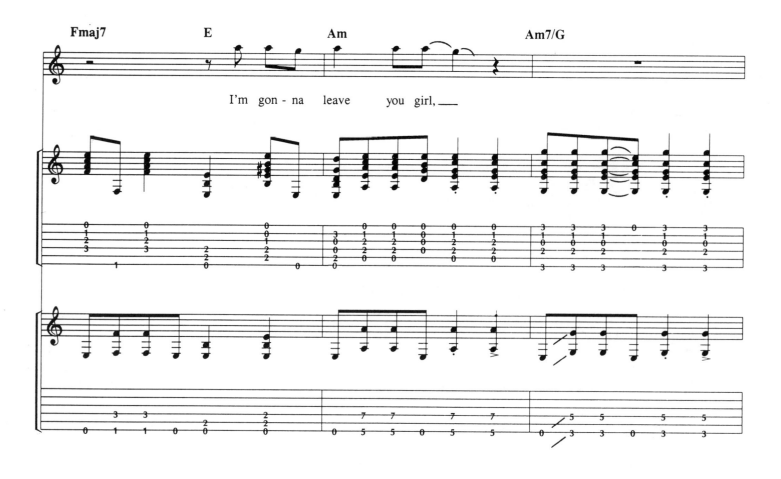

I'm gon - na leave you girl, ___

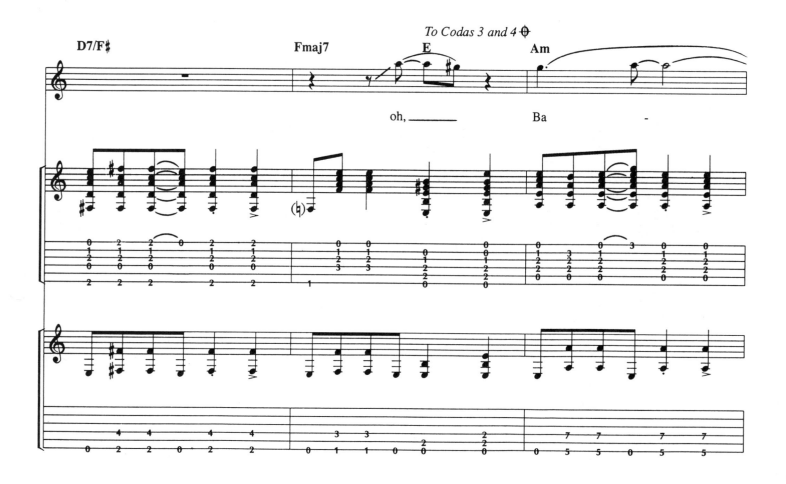

oh, _____ Ba -

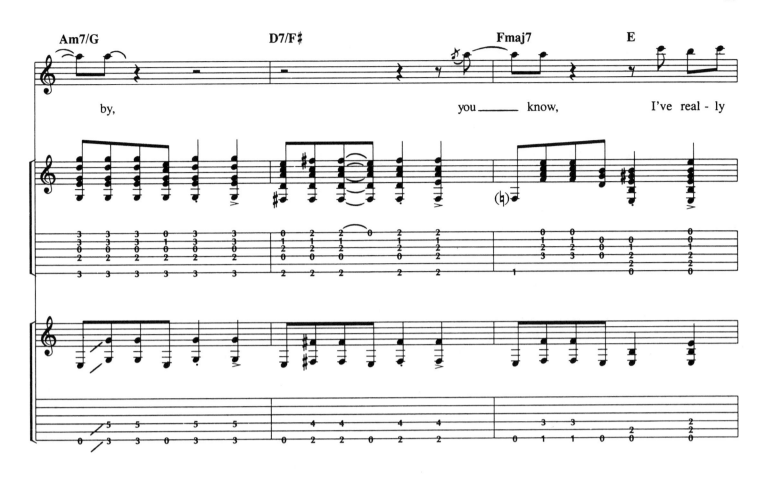

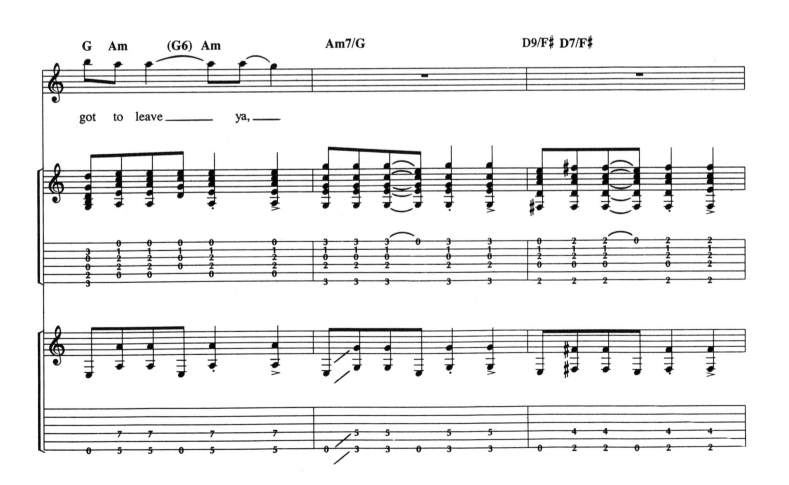

Coda 2

used to do.___

Acoustic Guitar Solo

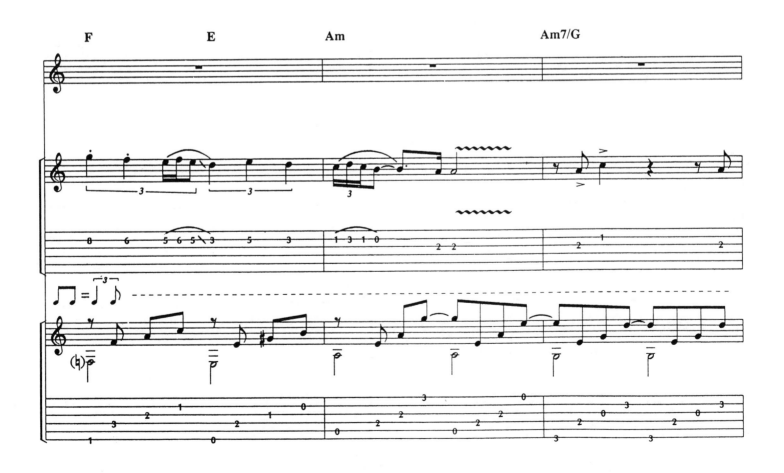

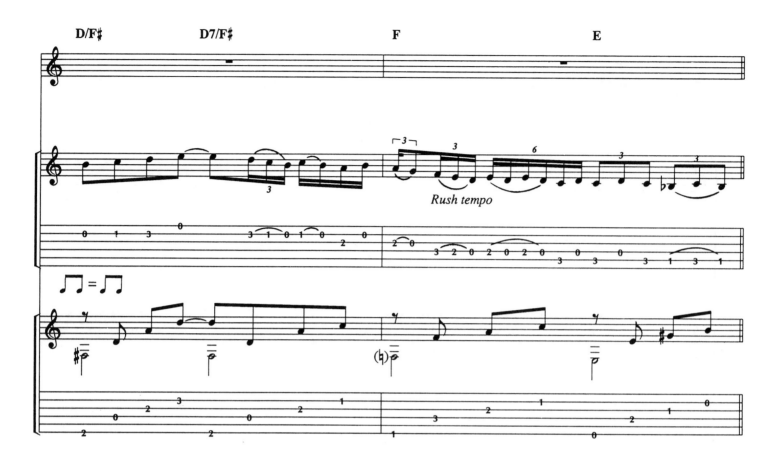

I know, _____ I know, _____ I know I'm nev-er nev-

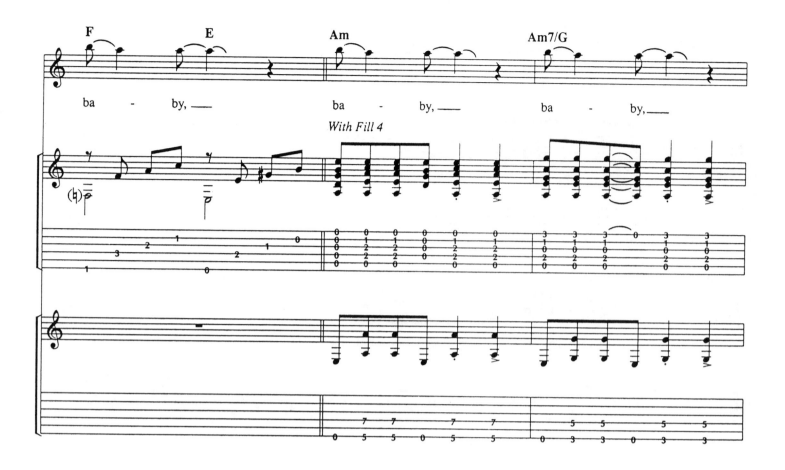

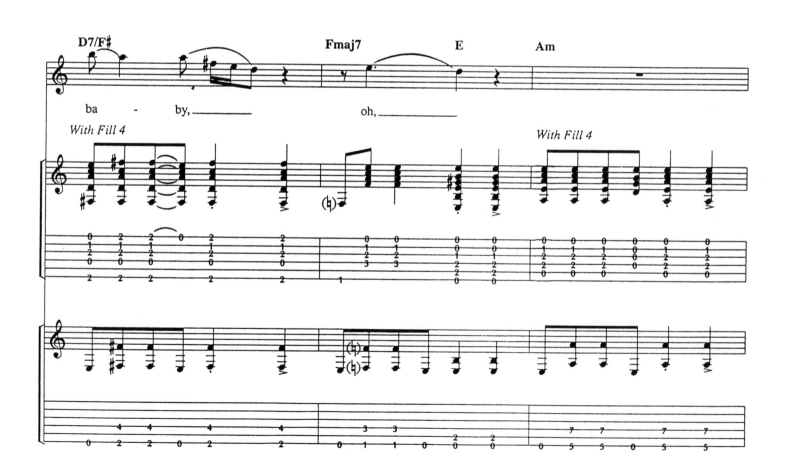

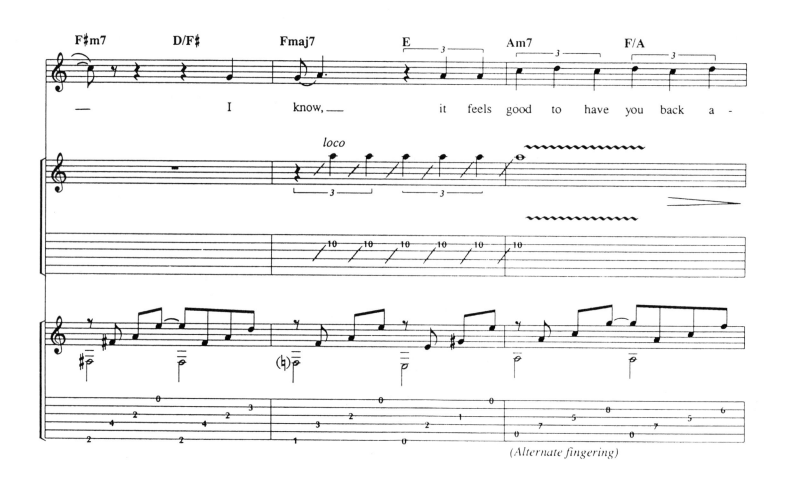

(Alternate fingering)

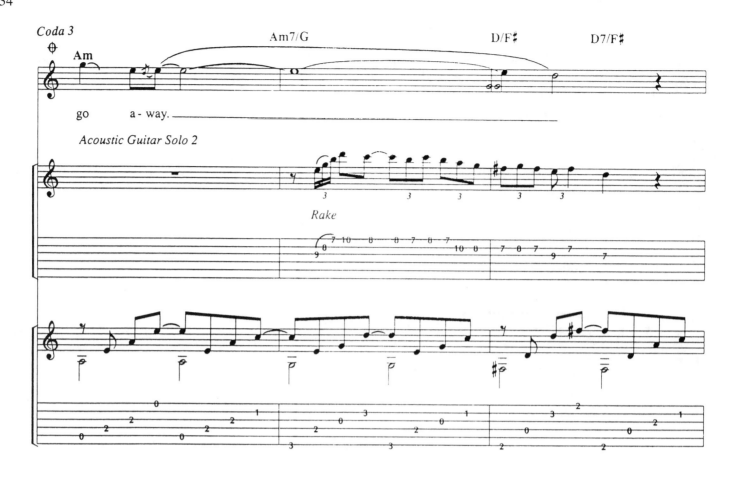

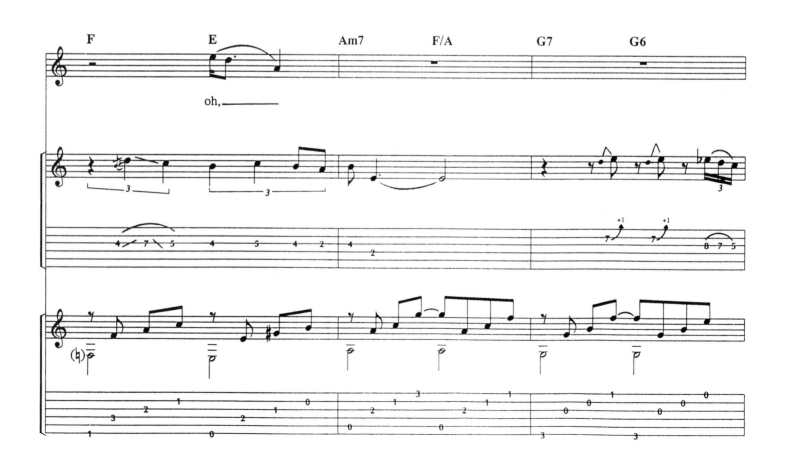

That's when it's cal-lin' me,

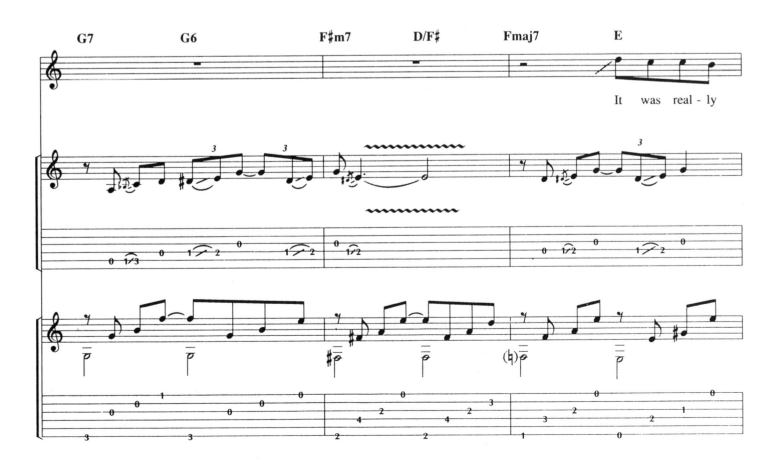

It was real-ly

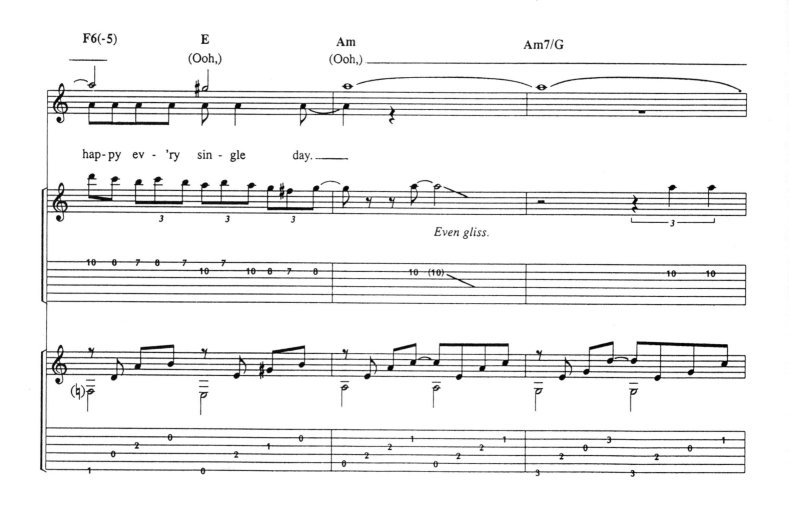

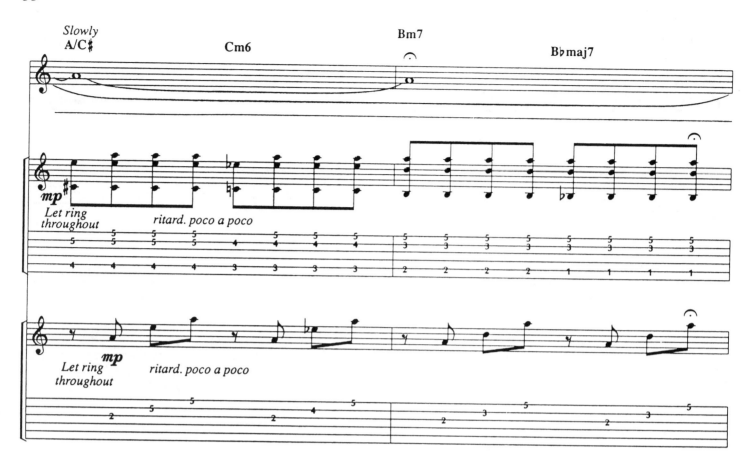

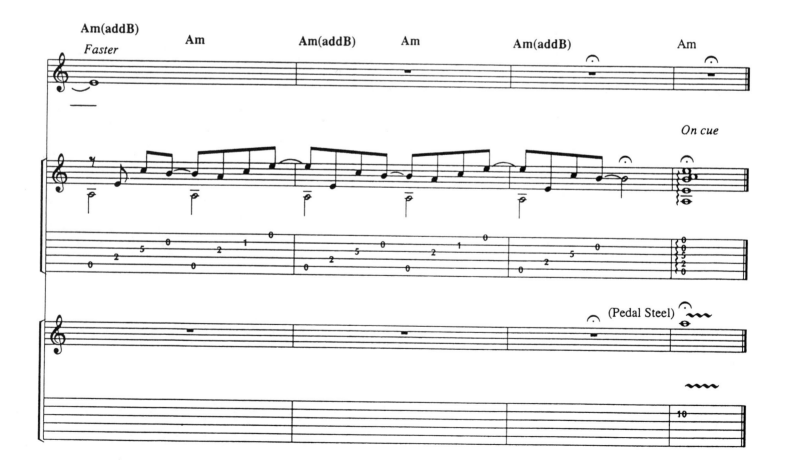

DAZED AND CONFUSED

Words and Music by
Jimmy Page

Electric Guitar (use neck-position pickup)

*Harm. with wah- wah throughout

Switch to treble pickup.

Verse 1:
N.C.

Been dazed and con - fused— for so long it's not true. Want-

Harm.

ed a wo - man, nev-er bar-gained for you.— Lots of peo-ple talk - in', few of them know—

Harm.

Harm.

* Rock wah-wah pedal simile to the following rhythm figure. (+ = treble position, 0 = bass position)

ritard.

soul   of   a   wo-man   was   cre - at - ed   be - low,_____   yeah._____

Upstemmed part played through fuzztone with octave effect (8va higher).
This can also be recreated with a pitch transposer.

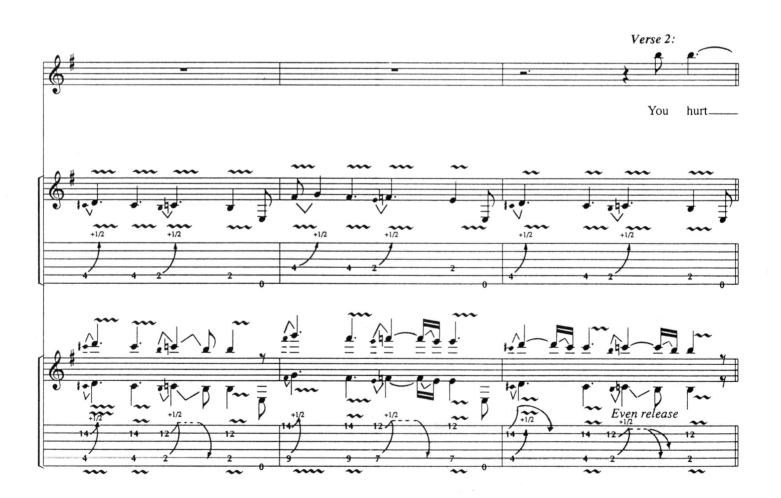

Verse 2:

You   hurt_____

and a-bused___ tell-in' all of your lies.___ Run 'round sweet ba - by, Lord,___ how they hyp-no-tize.__

Sweet lit-tle ba - by, I don't know where you been.__ Gon - na love you ba - by, here I come a -

gain.___

*Upstemmed part with 8va fuzz

Ev - 'ry

Verse 3:

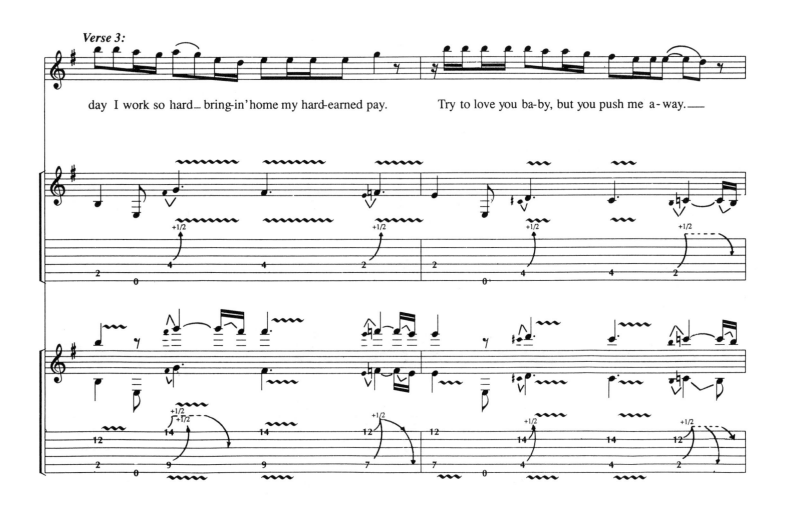

day I work so hard— bring-in' home my hard-earned pay.   Try to love you ba-by, but you push me a-way.—

Don't know where you're go-in', I don't know just where you've been; sweet lit-tle ba-by, I want you a -

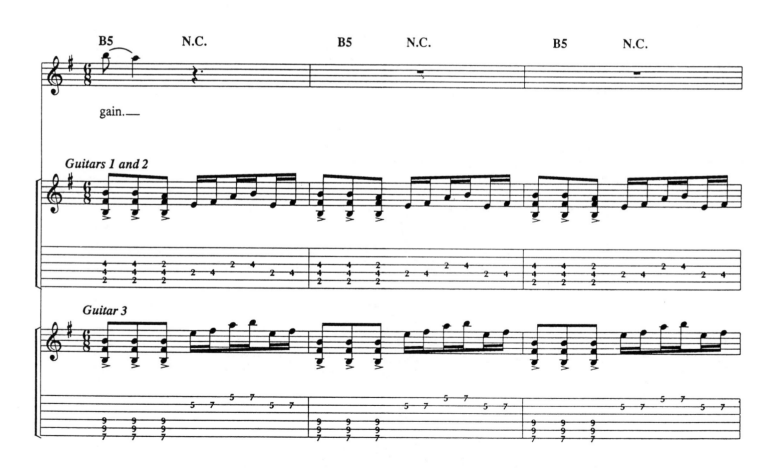

gain.

B5   N.C.   B5   N.C.   B5   N.C.

Guitars 1 and 2

Guitar 3

ah,_____ ah,

ah,_____ (ah)____

+1/2 -   Even gliss.

ah,_____

div.   Even gliss.

* Overdubbed fill. Tremelo with bow and wah wah.

ah,   ah,   ah.

Continue tremelo with bow.

yeah!   Al - right!

With wah-wah

Guitar Solo

Ah,   ah,   ah,   ah,   ah,   ah,

ah,   ah,   ah,   ah,   ah.

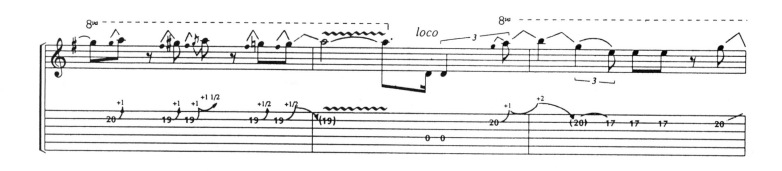

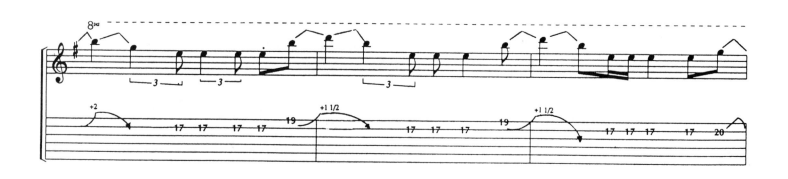

oh ____ don't leave me so con - fused, ____

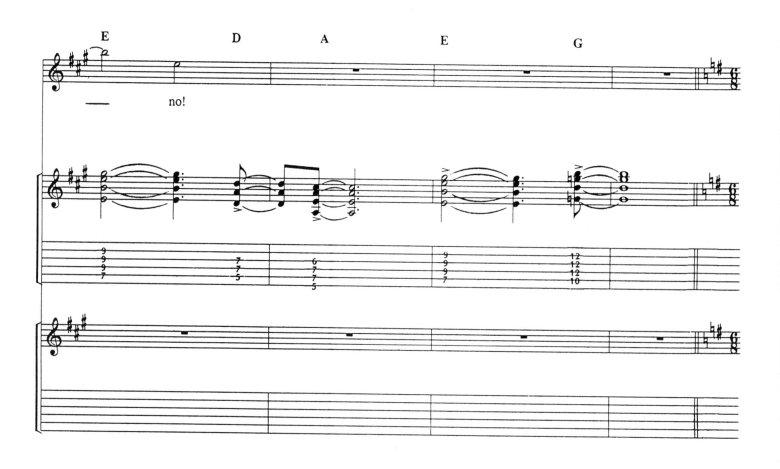

no!

Oh,

Guitar 1

Guitar 2

ba - by!____

Upstemmed part with 8va fuzz.

Been

dazed and con-fused for so long, it's not true,___ want-ed a wo-man nev-er bar-gained for you.___

Take it ea-sy ba-by, let them say what they will.—(Will your) tongue wag so much when I send you the

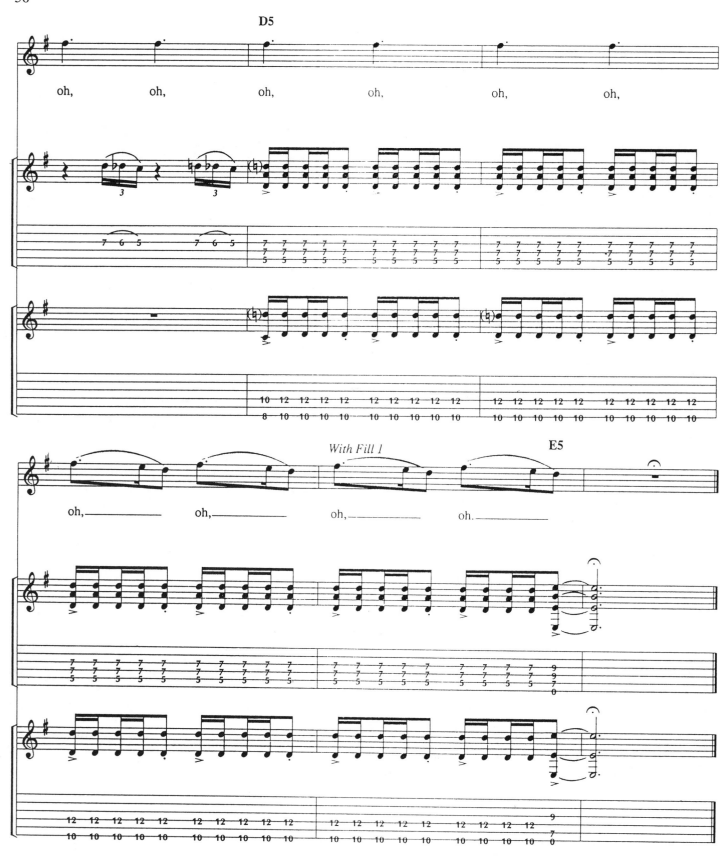

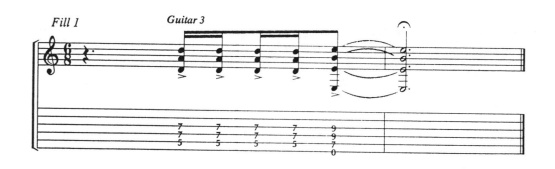

COMMUNICATION BREAKDOWN

Words and Music by
Jimmy Page, John Paul Jones and John Bonham

58

Verse 1:

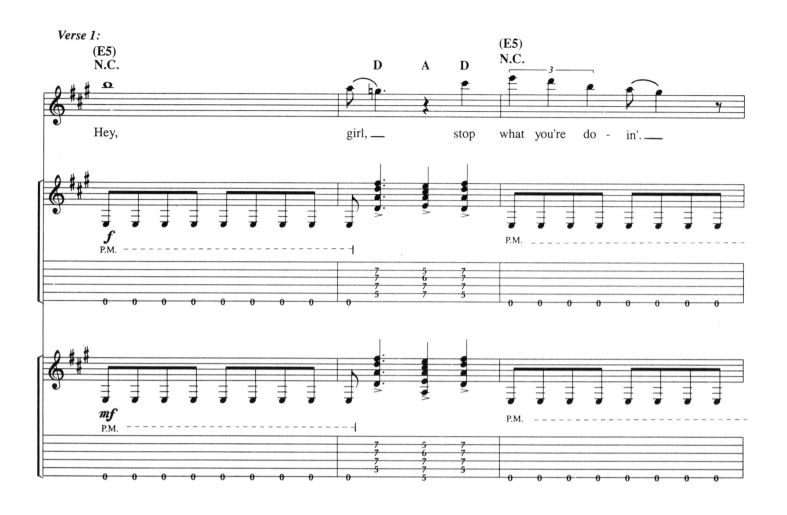

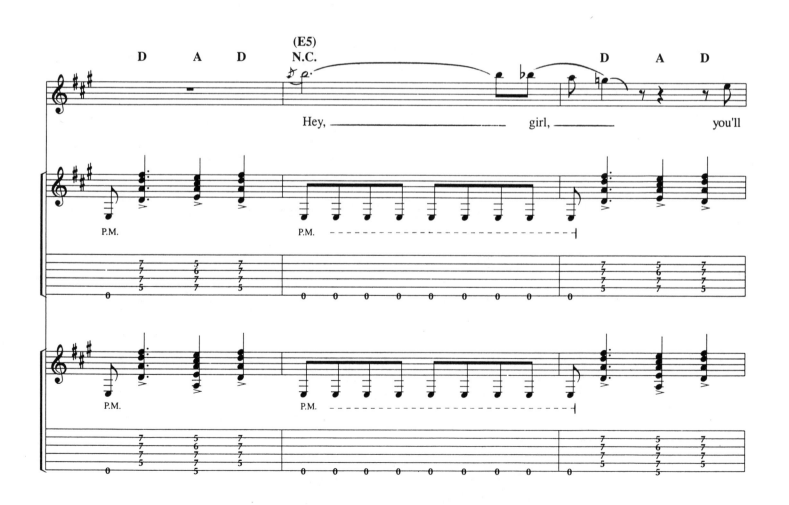

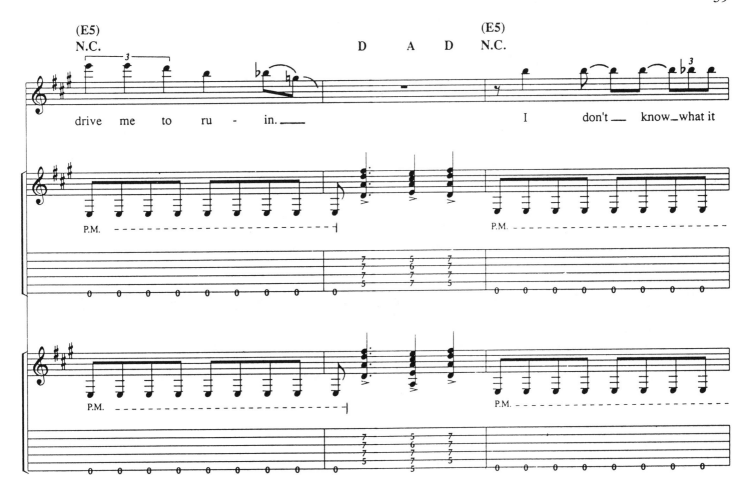

drive me to ru - in. ___ I don't ___ know ___ what it

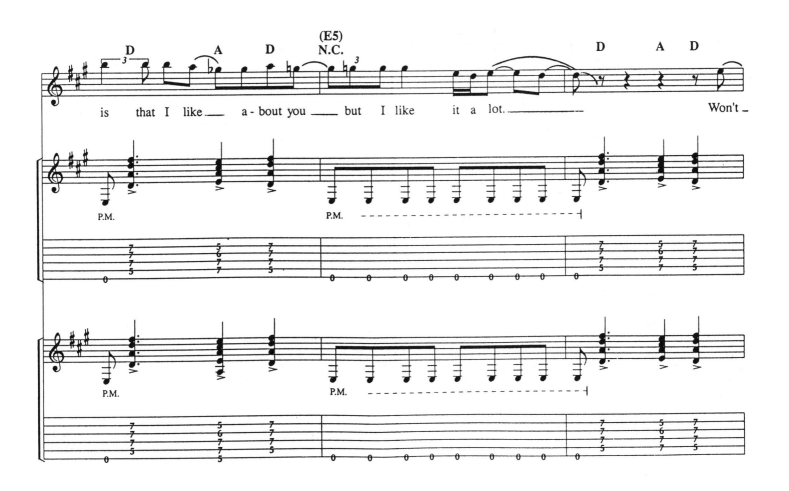

is that I like ___ a - bout you ___ but I like it a lot. ___ Won't ___

you let me hold you, let me feel your lov-in' charms.

Chorus:

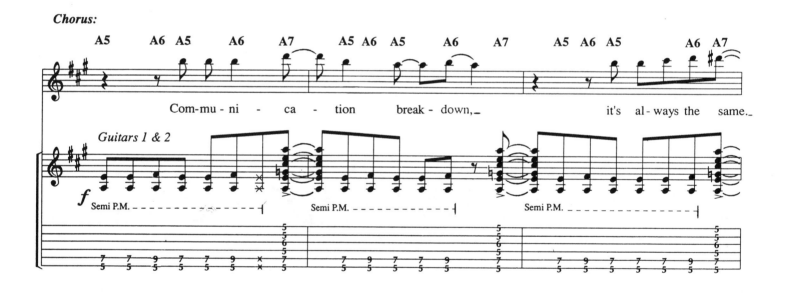

Com-mu-ni-ca-tion break-down, it's al-ways the same.

Guitars 1 & 2

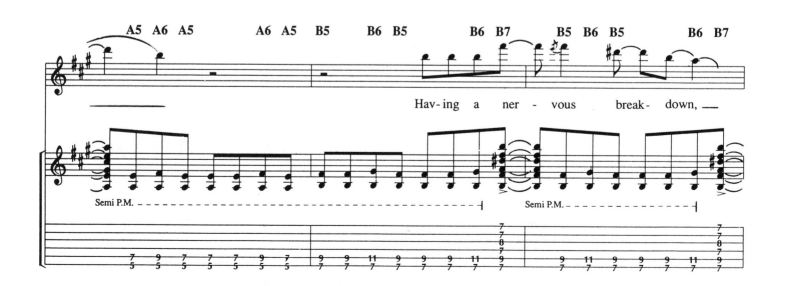

Hav-ing a ner-vous break-down,

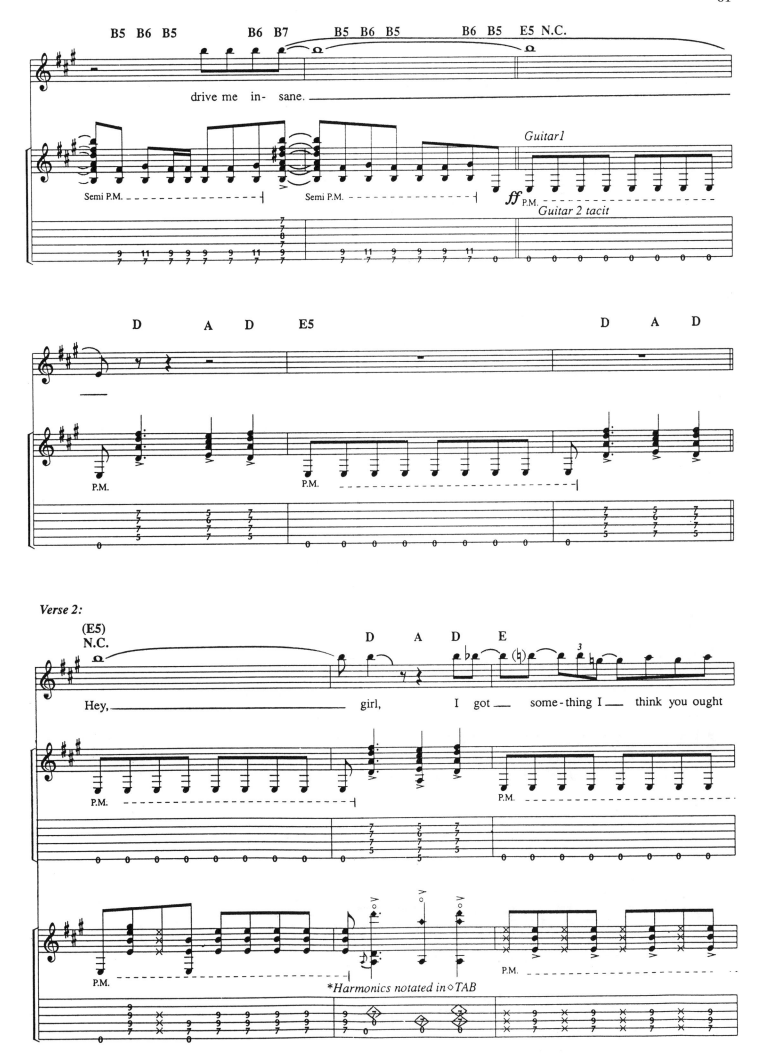

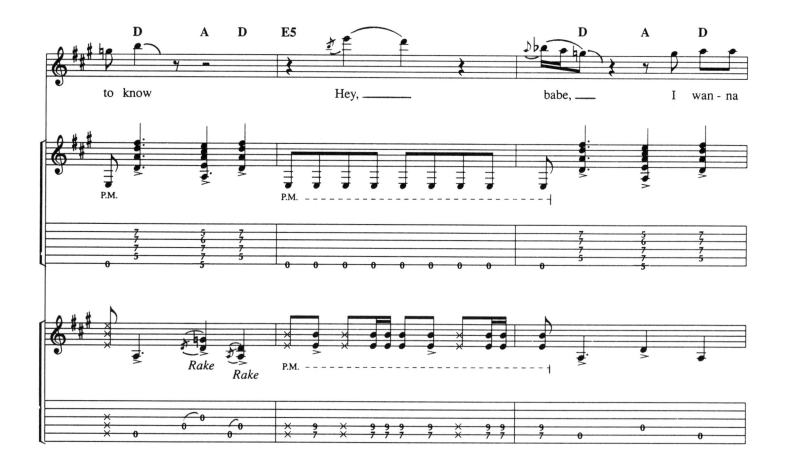

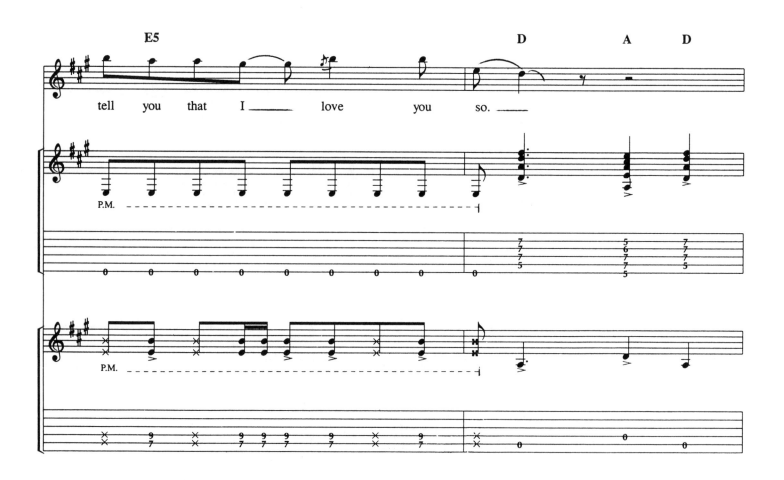

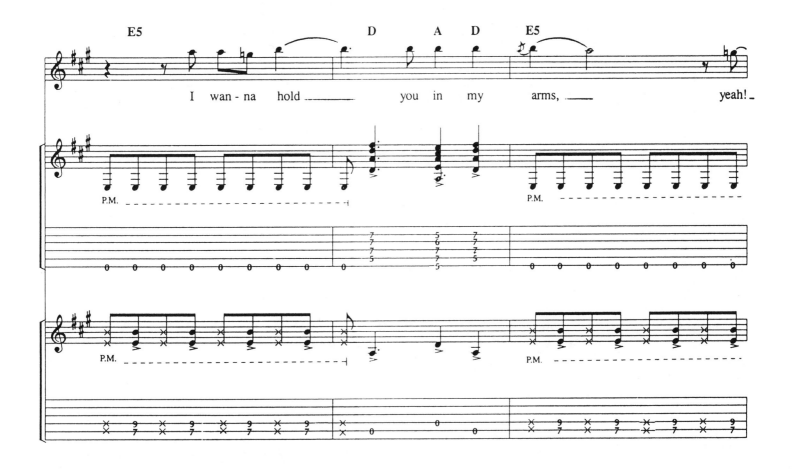

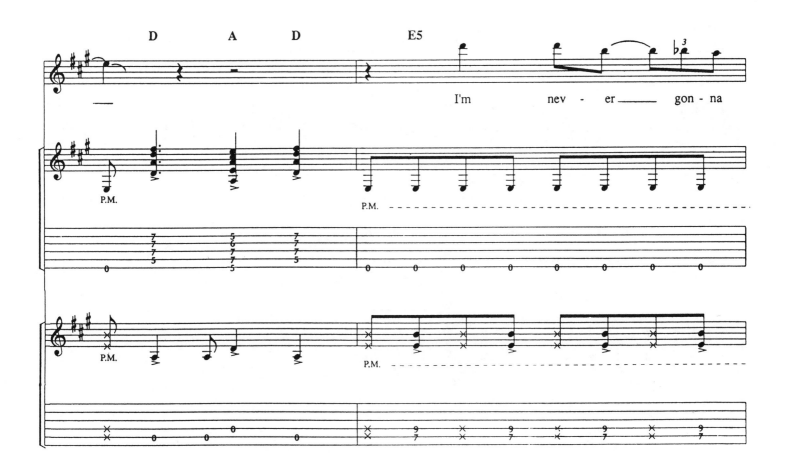

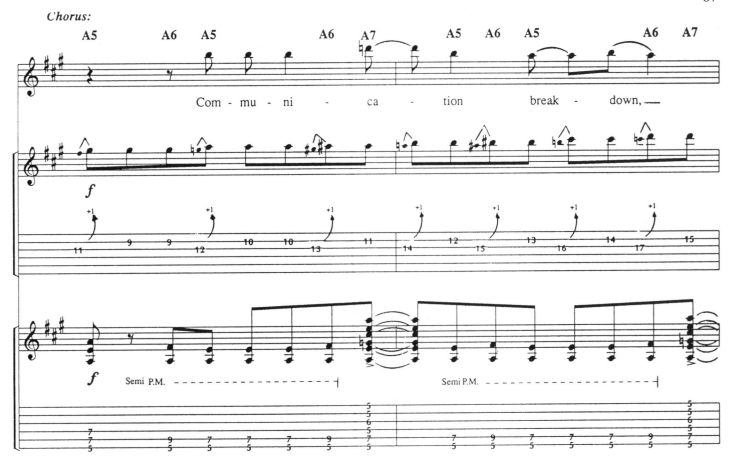

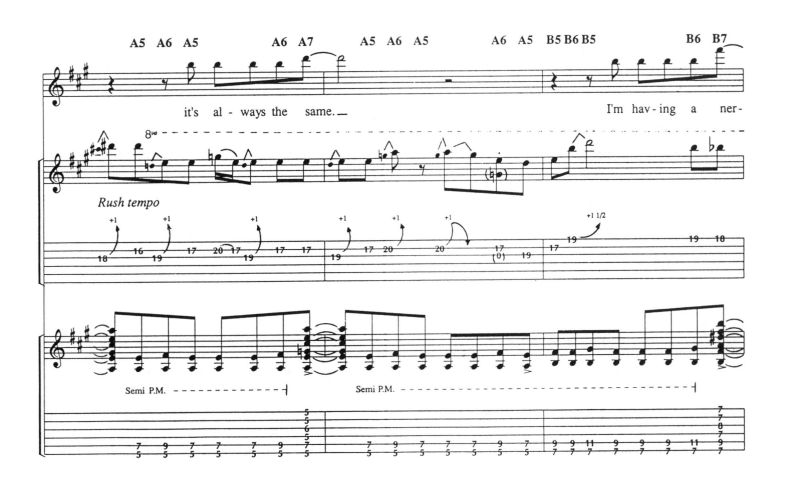

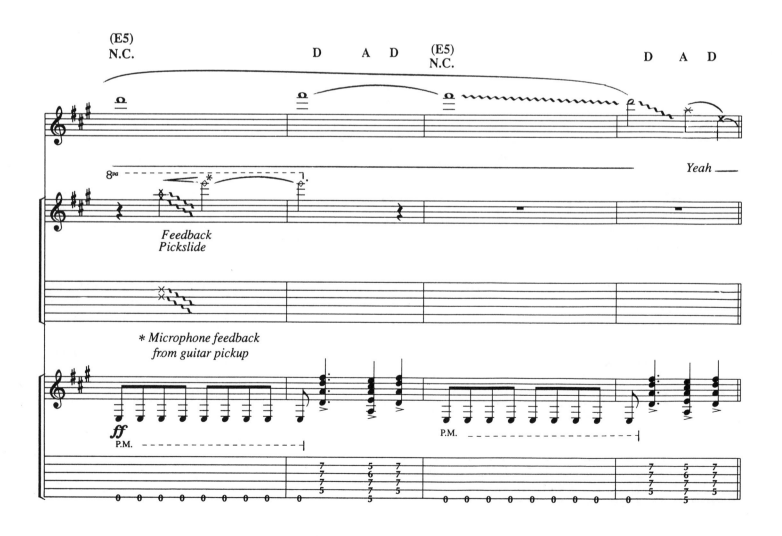

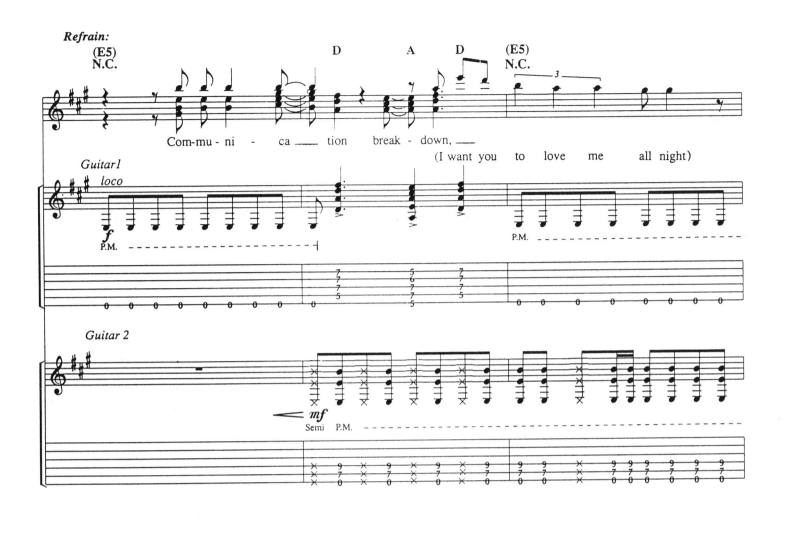

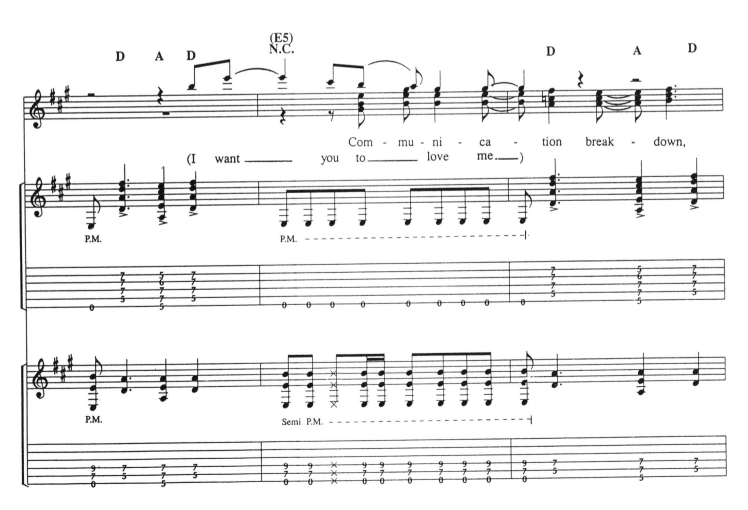

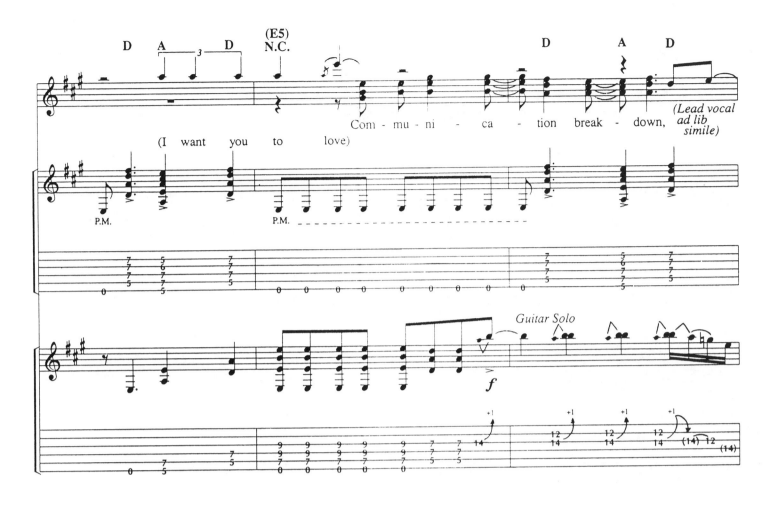

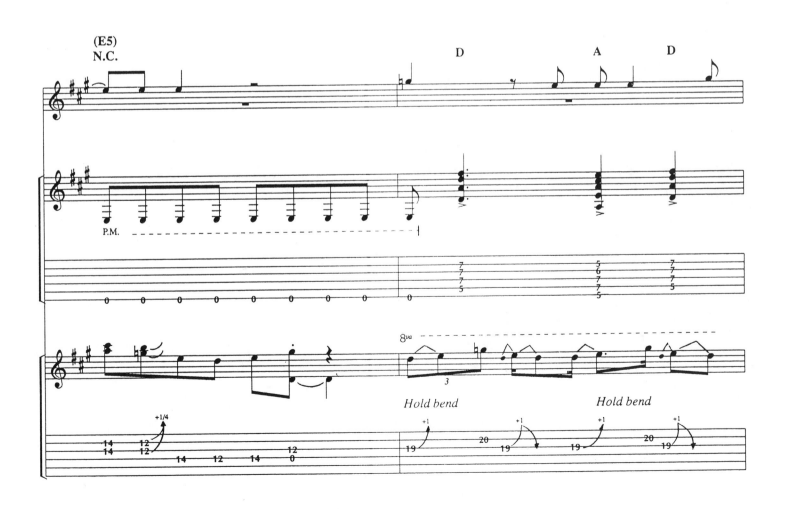

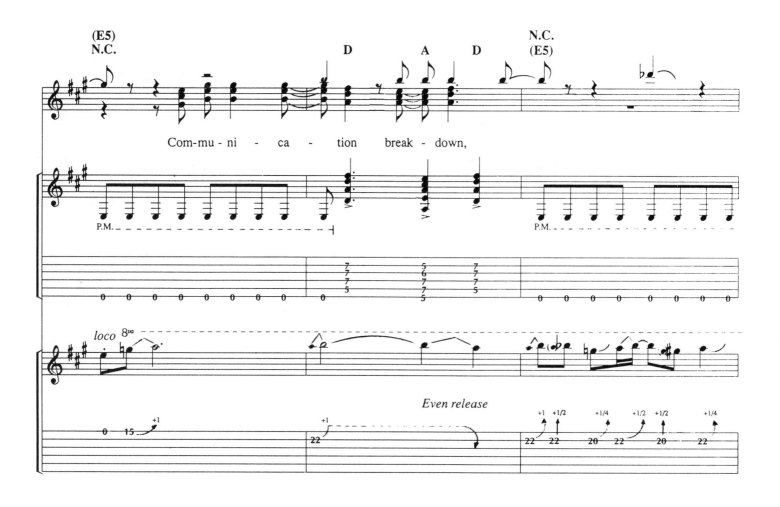

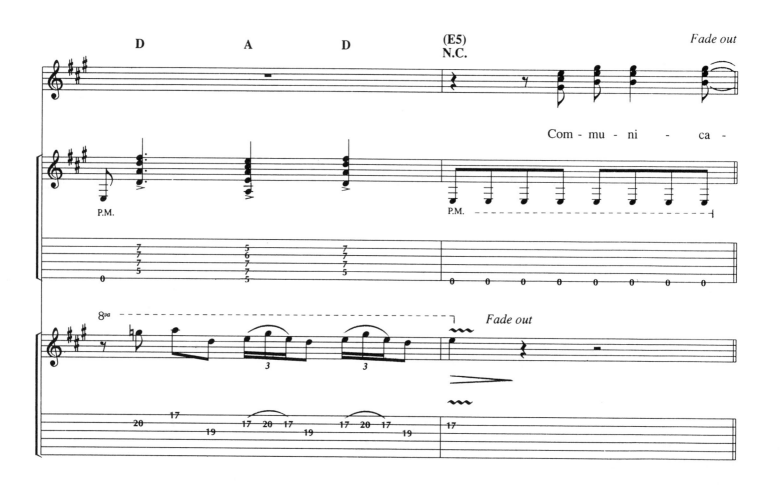

WHOLE LOTTA LOVE

Words and Music by
Jimmy Page, Robert Plant, John Paul Jones,
John Bonham and Willie Dixon

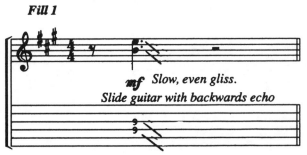

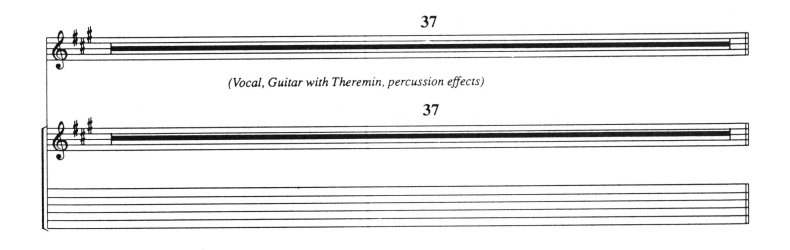

37

(Vocal, Guitar with Theremin, percussion effects)

37

Electric Guitar 2

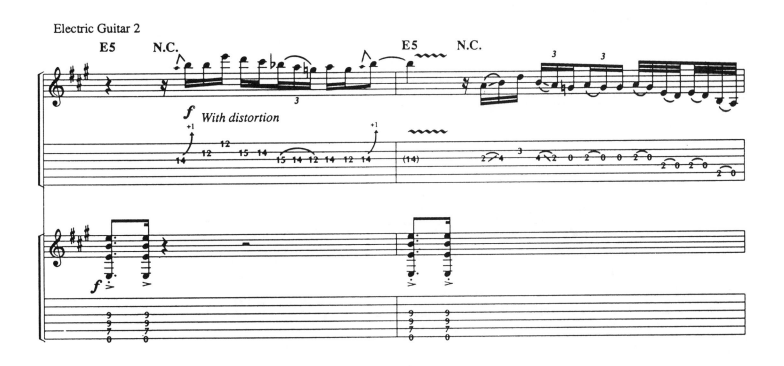

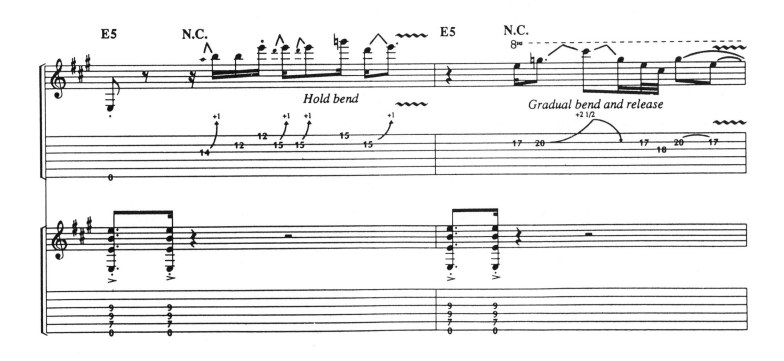

WHAT IS AND WHAT SHOULD NEVER BE

Words and Music by
Jimmy Page and Robert Plant

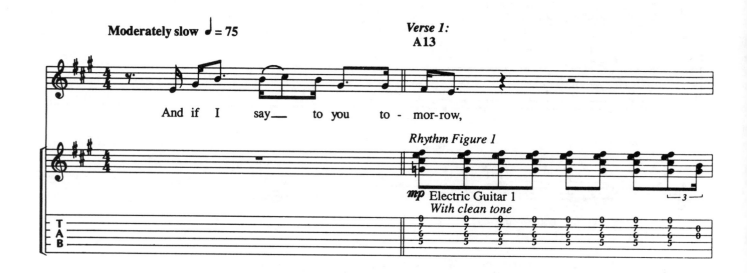

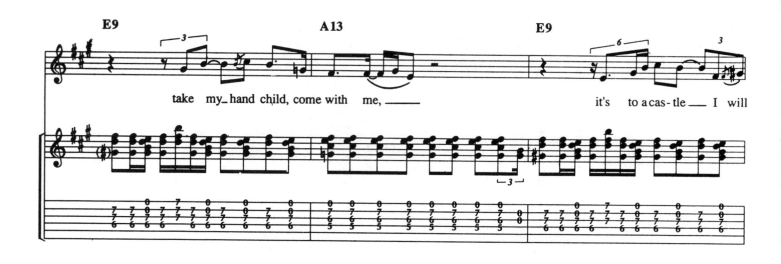

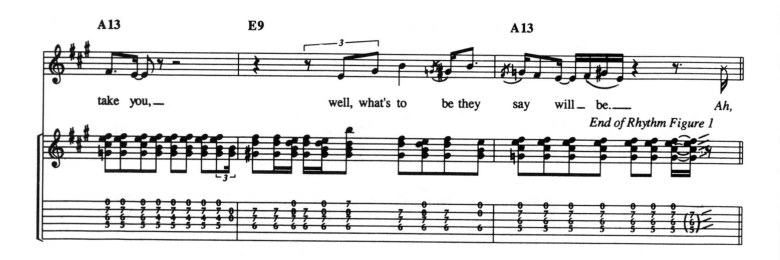

IMMIGRANT SONG

Words and Music by
Jimmy Page and Robert Plant

Note: All chord names reflect composite guitar harmonies.
**With amplifier vibrato set to 16th note pulse.*

Verse 1:

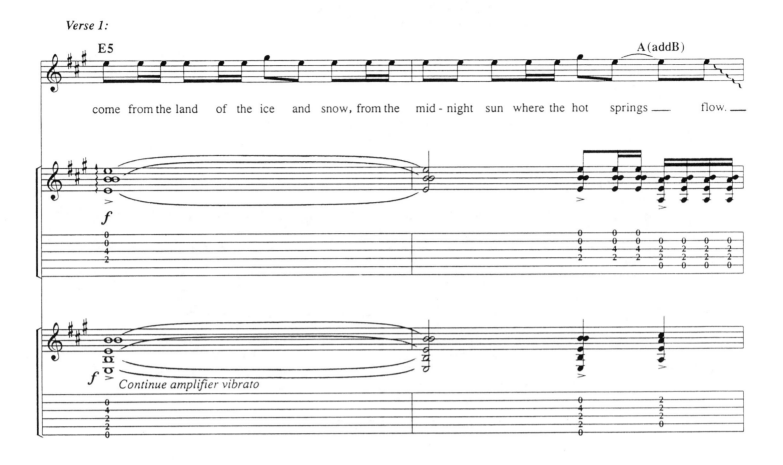

come from the land   of the ice   and snow, from the   mid - night sun where the hot   springs ___   flow. ___

— Ham-mer   of ___ the   gods,   will drive   our ships   to new ___

Guitar 1

Guitar 3   *(Guitar 2 tacet)*

** *Muted scratch/strum-roughly parallels the bass part.*

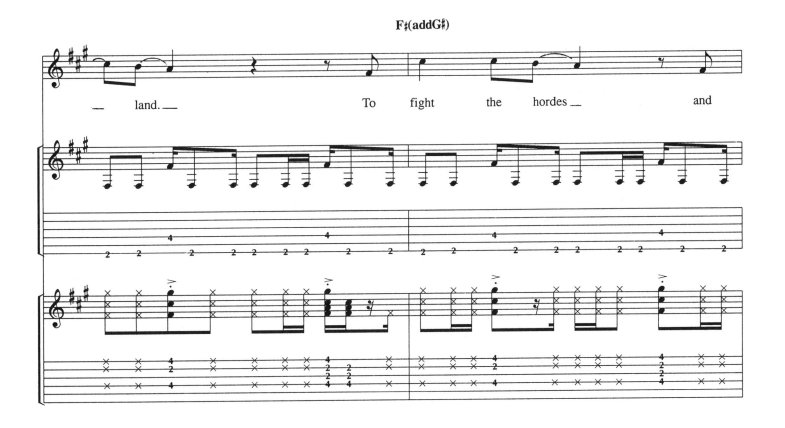

Return 16th note amplifier vibrato

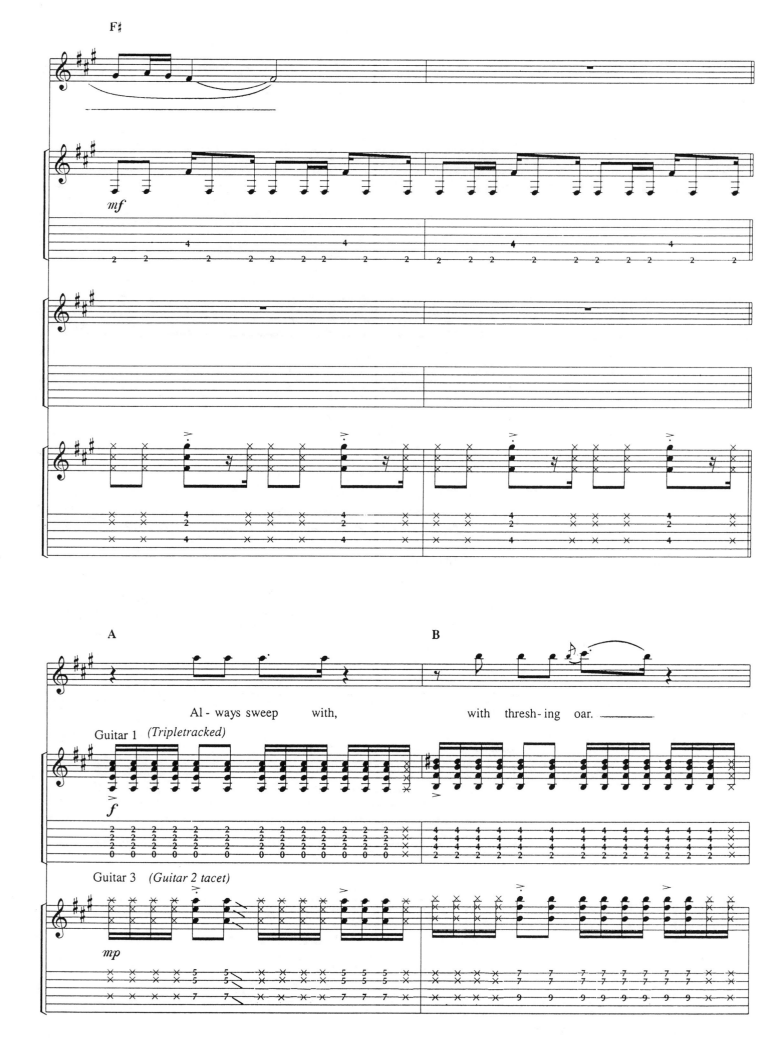

C

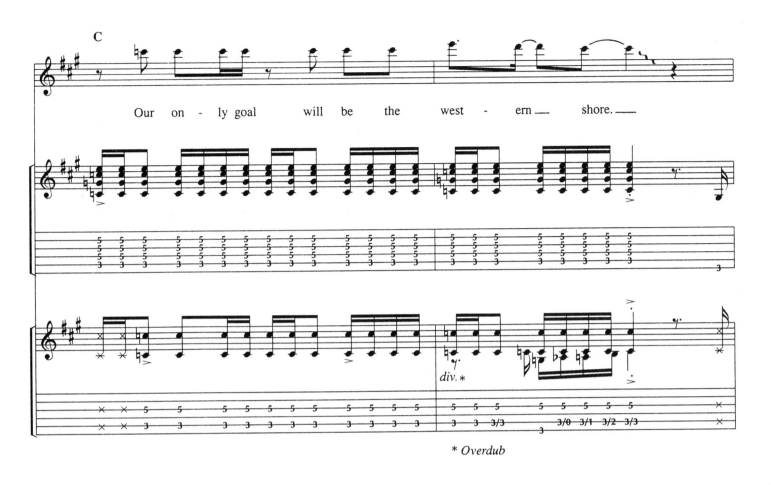

Our on - ly goal will be the west - ern ___ shore. ___

div. *

* *Overdub*

(Intro:)

F♯(addG♯)

mf

Ah, _____

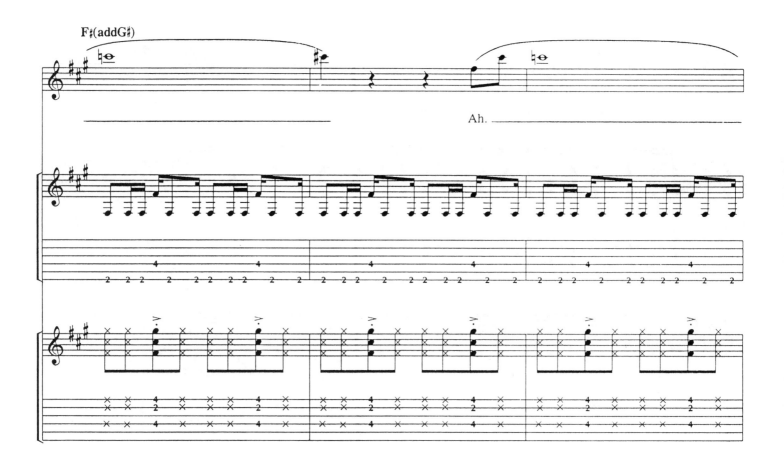

F#(addG#)

Ah.

Verse 2:

A5　　　　E5

We come from the land of the ice and snow, from the

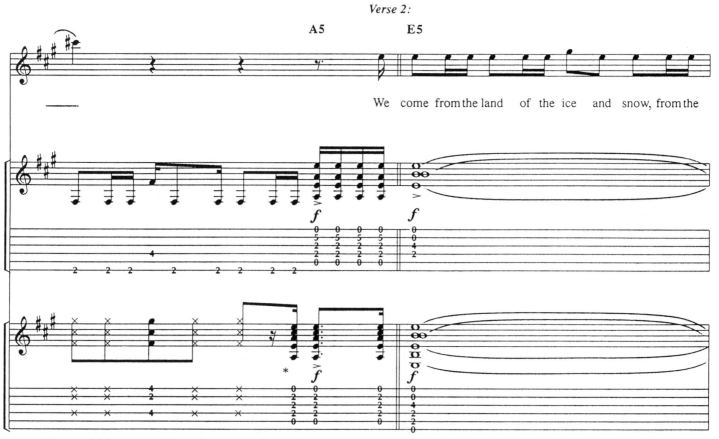

* Return 16th note amplifier vibrato with Guitar 2.

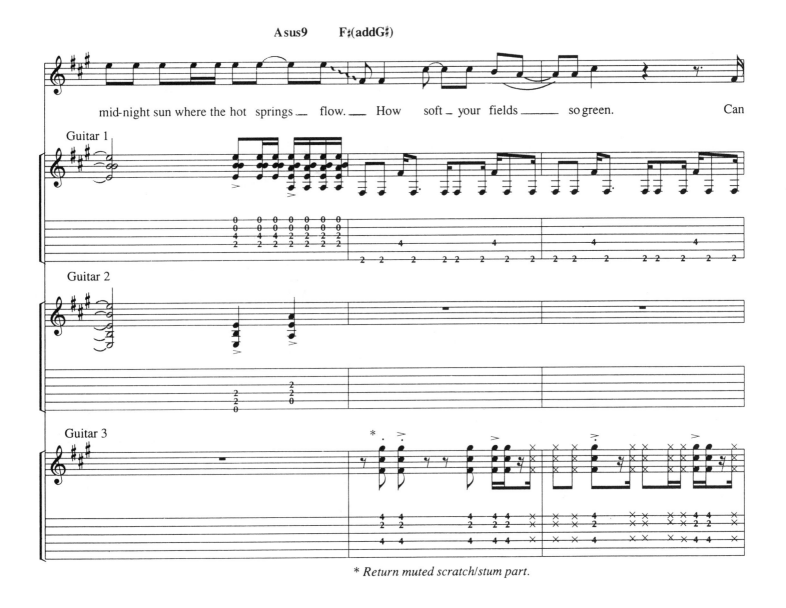

mid-night sun where the hot springs flow. How soft your fields so green. Can

* Return muted scratch/stum part.

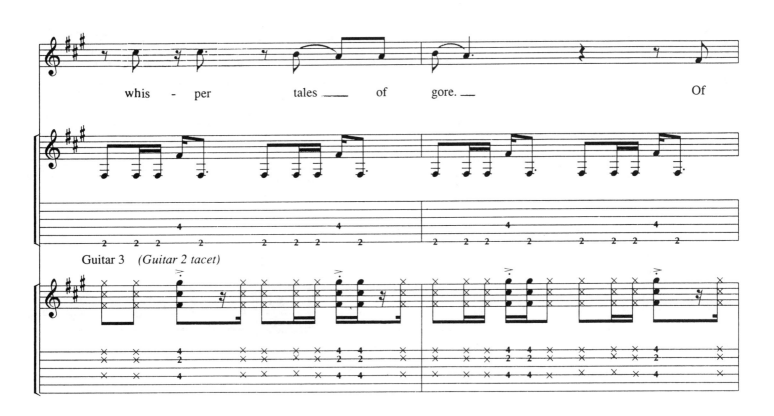

whis - per tales of gore. Of

how we calmed ... the tides of war. ___ We are ___ your

*Return 16th note amplifier vibrato.

ov - er Lords. ___

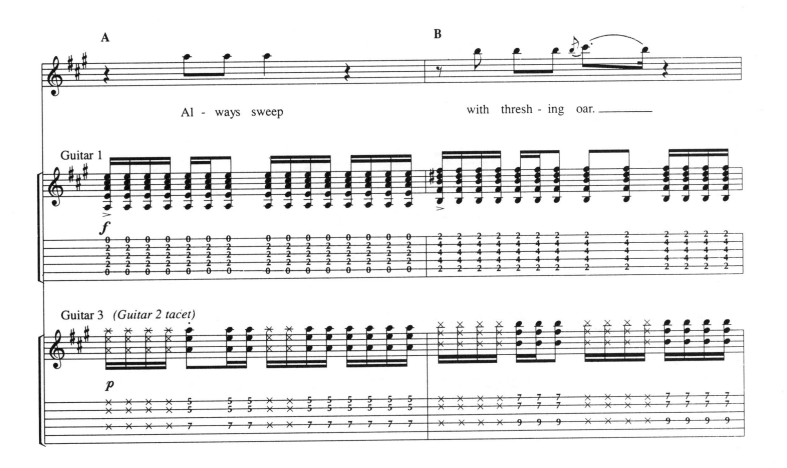

A Al - ways sweep   **B** with thresh - ing oar. _____

C Our on - ly goal will be the west - ern _ shore. __

* Additional Guitar in unison with
original (treble pick-up with distortion.)

F#(addG#)

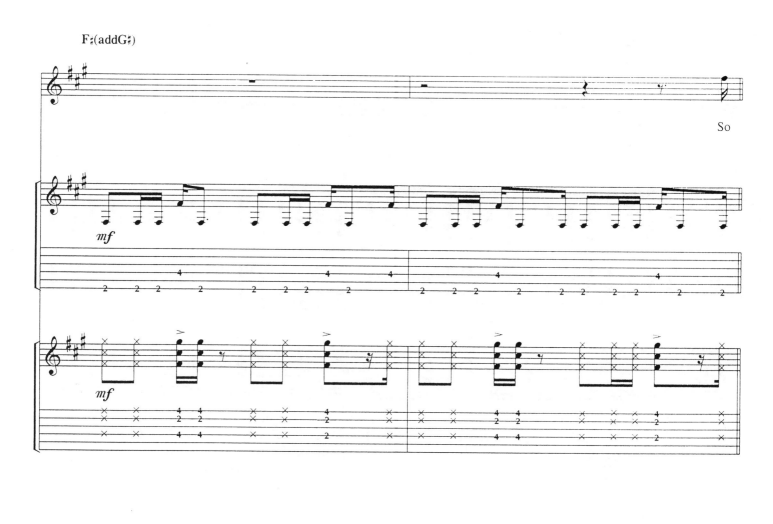

So

now you'd bet-ter stop, ___ and re-build all ___ your ru-ins. For

Upstemmed part on beats 3&4: additional guitar fill.

peace and trust can __ win the day, de - spite of all your __ los - ing. __

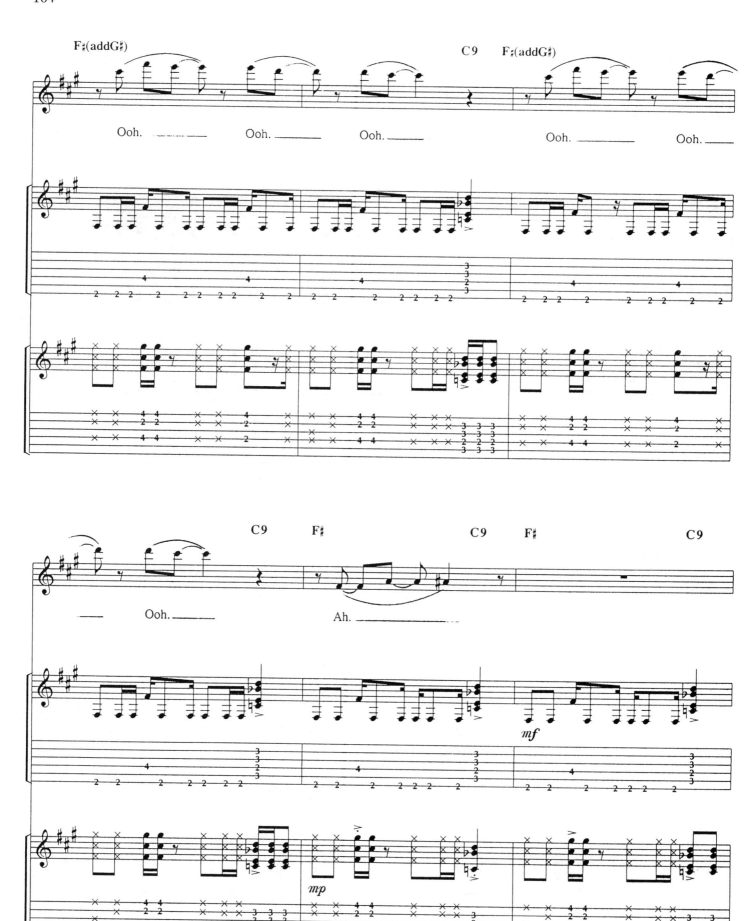

SINCE I'VE BEEN LOVING YOU

Words and Music by
Jimmy Page, Robert Plant and John Paul Jones

*Les Paul: volume is varied throughout (approximate: neck = 10, bridge = 7).

**Chords implied by the organ bass pedals.

***Chords stated or implied by the organ. Passing chords in parenthesis. This Fm7 can also be
thought of as Ab/F. This chord voicing approach is used on the organ throughout the song.

****Both pickups: neck = 10, bridge = 7.

*Bridge (lead) pickup only = 10
**Both pickups: neck = 10, bridge = 7.

*Add fuzztone.

**Interior strings are muted with left hand.

*Fuzztone out.

**Position hand at first fret.

***Re-position hand at third fret.

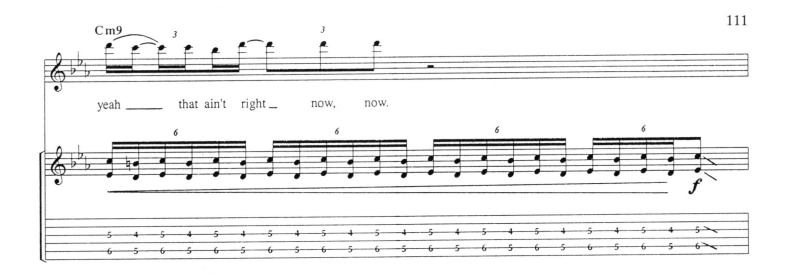

yeah _____ that ain't right _ now, now.

Since _____ I've been lov-in' you, _ I'm a-bout to lose _ my wor-ried

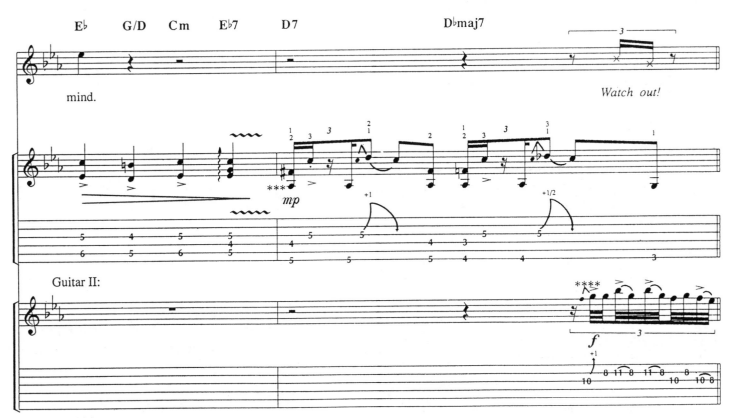

mind.

Watch out!

Guitar II:

*Add fuzztone.

**Third string muted with fretting hand. Open second string occurs later
in the song and may be a guitar error, but is notated for accuracy.

***Fifth string muted with fretting hand. See suggested fingering. Fuzztone out.

****Bridge pickup: 10, with medium fuzz.

*Add fuzztone.
**Downstrums only through measure eleven.

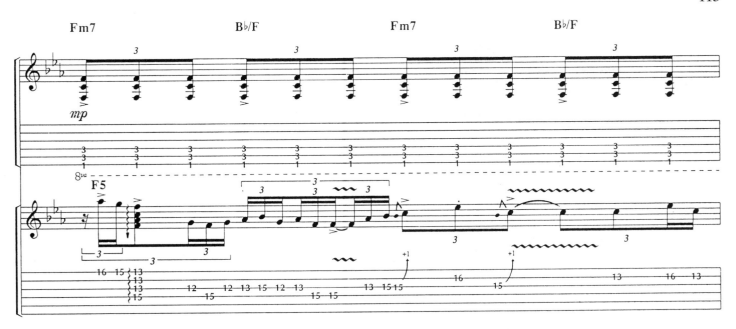

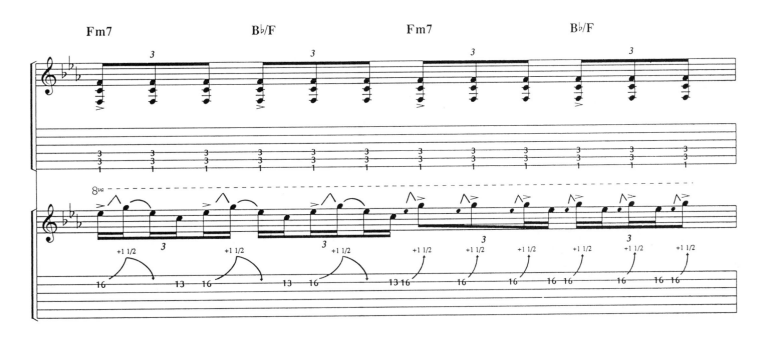

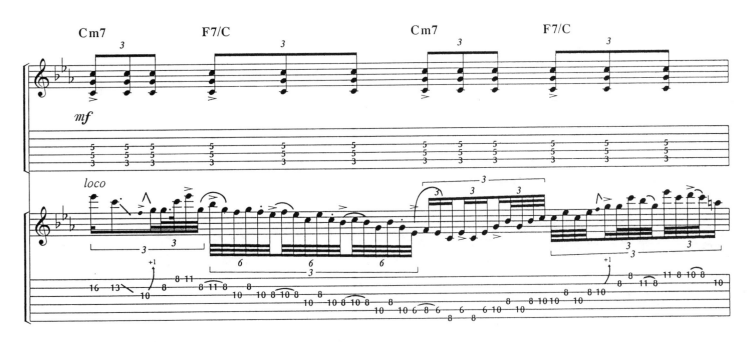

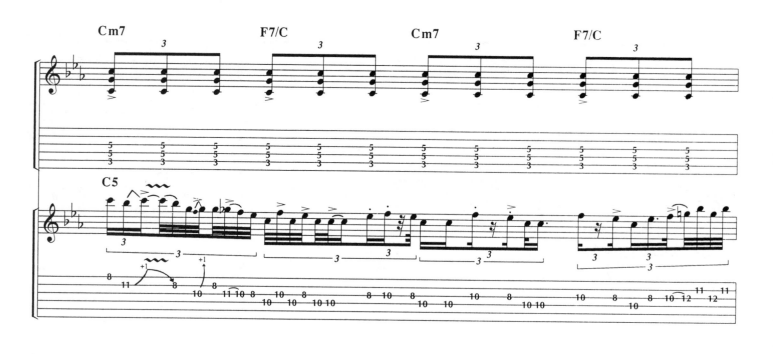

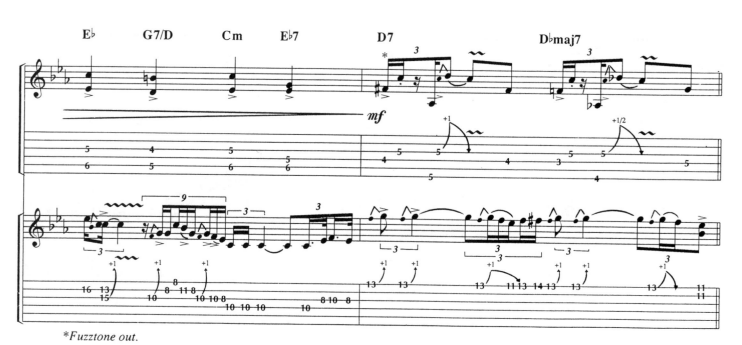

Fuzztone out.

*Downstrums. Add fuzztone.

one of them new fan-gled, new___ fan-gled back door men, yeah, yeah, yeah, yeah, yeah, yeah.

I've been a' work-ing from sev - en, sev - en, sev - en to e -

le - ven ev - 'ry night it kind - a makes my life a drag,___ (a

*Notes and lyrics in parentheses are whispered here.

*Fuzztone out.
**Slide down and up repeatedly.

BLACK DOG

Words and Music by
Jimmy Page, Robert Plant and John Paul Jones

*Guitar 1 (Right channel) is in downstems and Guitar 2 (Left channel) is in upstems.

**This pitch is from a tape effect and not playable. See Performance Notes.

***Enter on drummer's cue.

****Guitar 2 enters and sustains its A5 chord into Verse 2, whereas
Guitar 1 plays it's A5 chord again on the downbeat of Verse 2.

*Guitar 1 is faded out in the first measure. (Simile for all verses)

**Guitar 2 joins Guitar 1 through Verse 3.

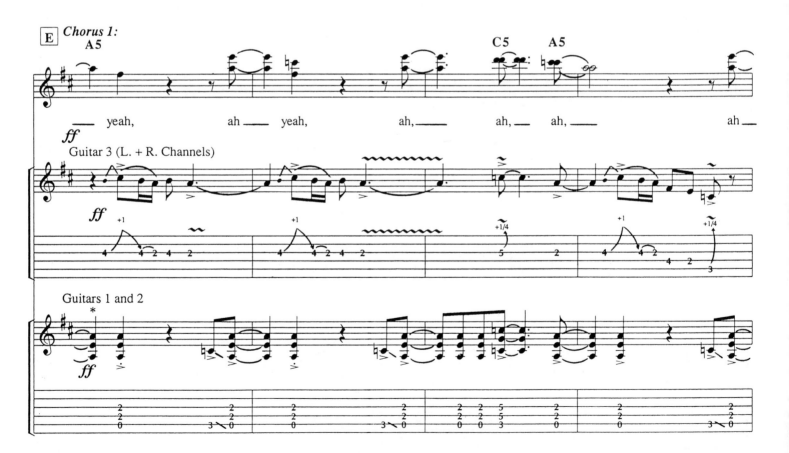

The Guitar 2 part omits the upper note of each power chord throughout the Chorus

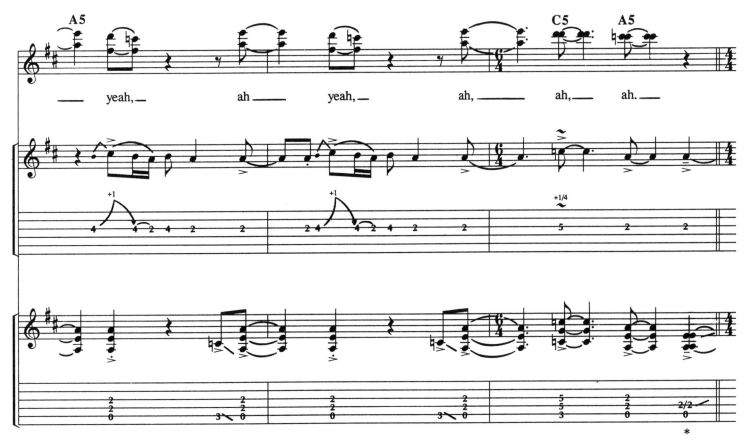

*Guitar 1 begins a slide up to A, while Guitar 2 repeats A5.

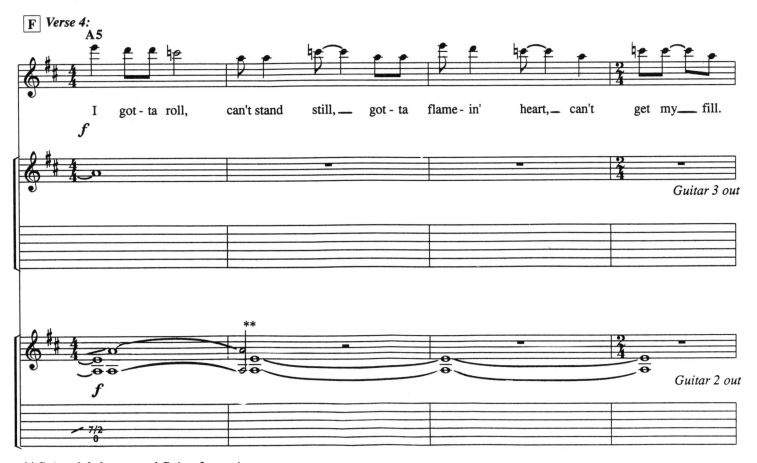

**Guitar 1 fades out and Guitar 2 sustains.

Eyes that shine,— burn-in' red,— dreams of you— all through my head.—

*Guitar 1 is faded out in the second measure.

Ah ah ah ah ah ah ah ah ah ah ah ah

**Guitar 1 is faded out in the second measure.

***Feedback harmonic

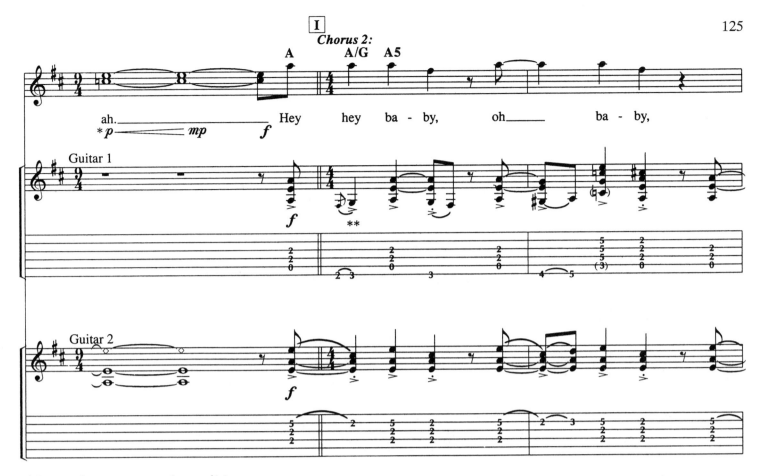

*Crescendo on upper note in vocal(e).
**Hammer on between thumb and second finger.

***Although these are the proper chords, various notes are emphasized each time they're strummed.
****The note E is played here by the Bass guitar only, throughout Choruses 2 and 3.

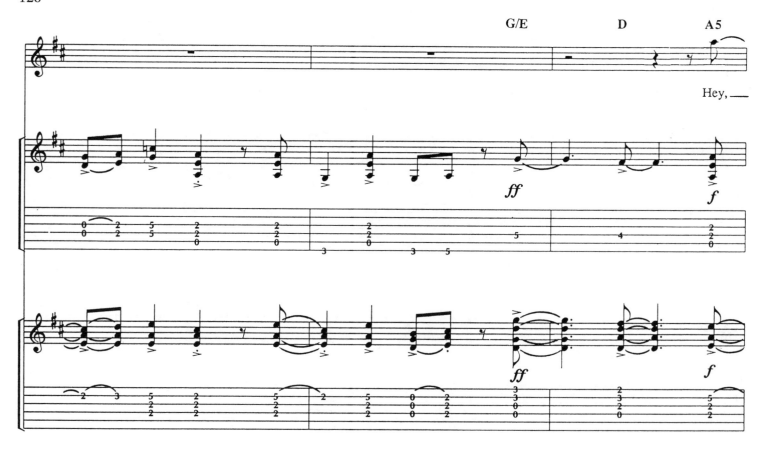

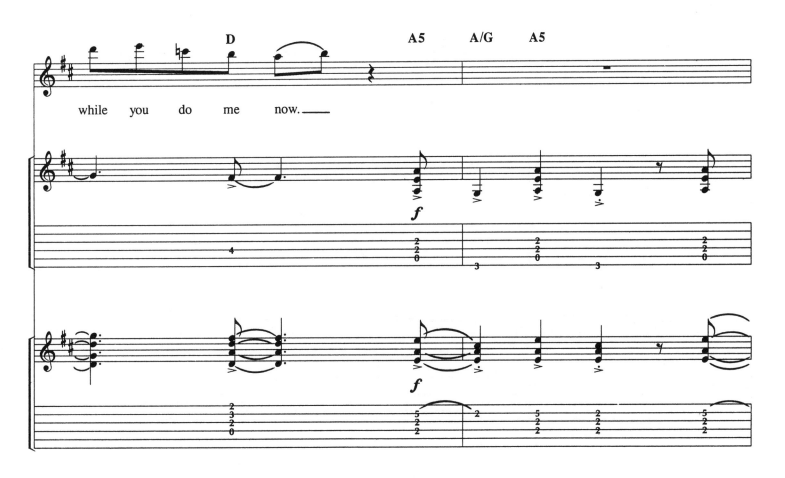

while you do me now.____

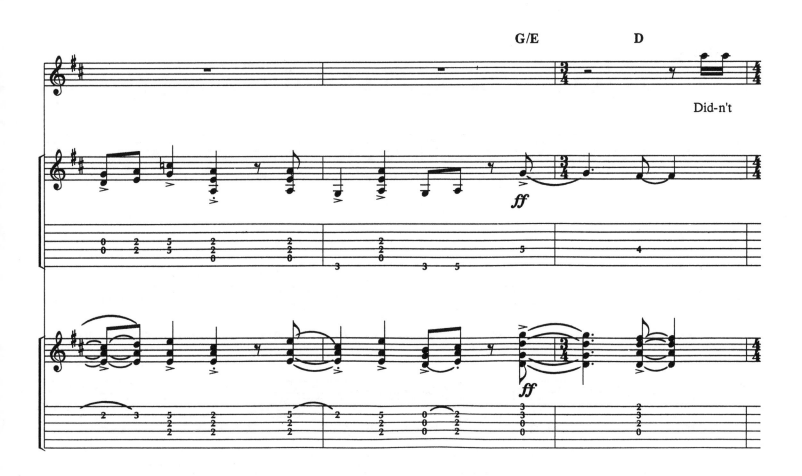

Did-n't

J *Verse 6:*
A5

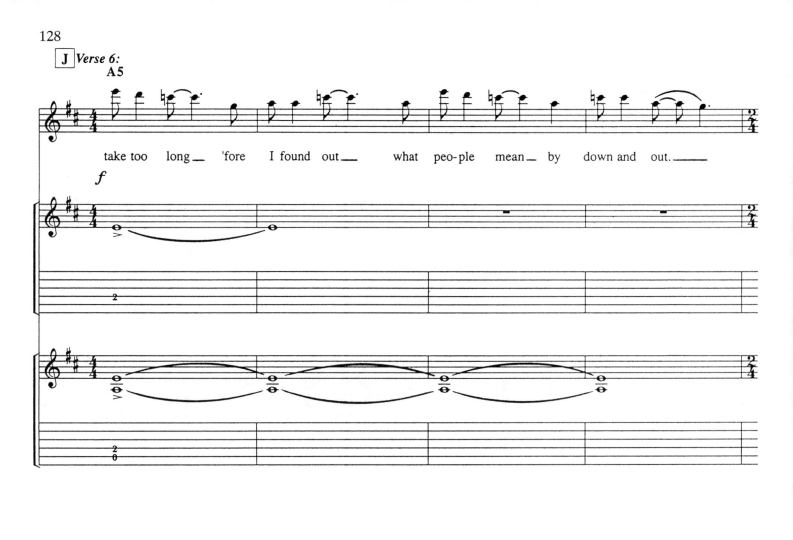

take too long___ 'fore I found out___ what peo-ple mean___ by down and out.___

N.C.

A5

Guitars 1 and 2

K *Verse 7:*
A5

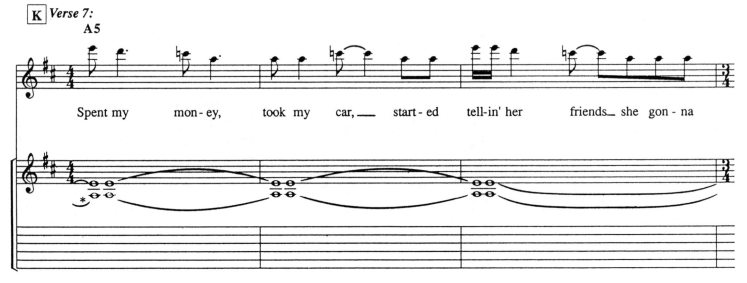

Spent my mon-ey, took my car,___ start-ed tell-in' her friends___ she gon-na

Guitar 1 fades out in measure 3.

be a star. _____

L *Verse 8:*

I don't know, — but I been told, — a big legged wom-an — ain't

got no soul. —

*Guitar 1 fades out in measure 2.

M A5 N.C.

*The Guitar 1 and 2 parts have been combined.
The Guitar 2 part omits the upper note of each power chord throughout the Chorus.

*Guitar 1 slides into A5 and fades out in measure 2, Guitar 2 sustains.

A5

P Verse 10:

A5

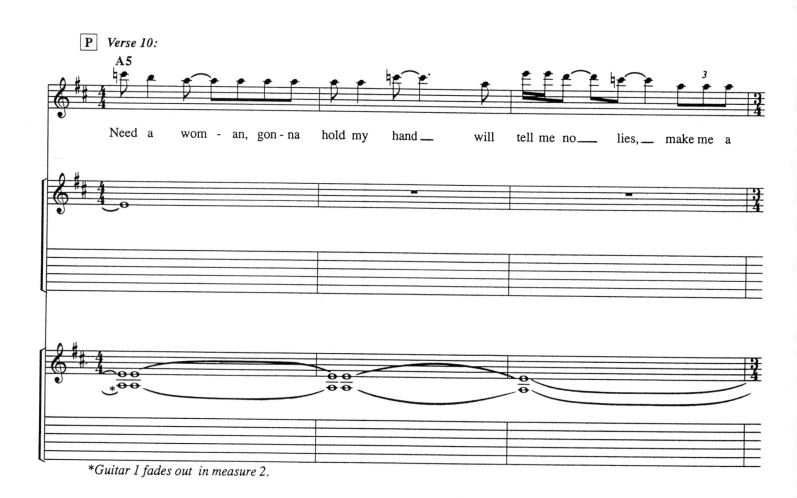

Need a wom - an, gon - na hold my hand___ will tell me no___ lies,___ make me a

*Guitar 1 fades out in measure 2.

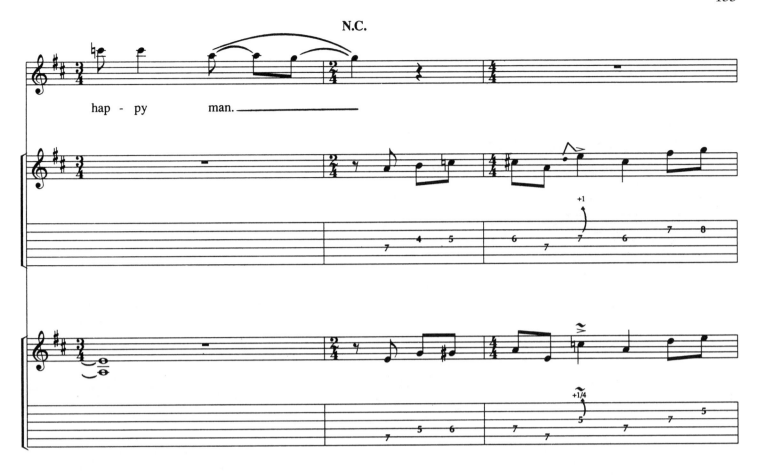

hap - py   man. _____

G Bridge:

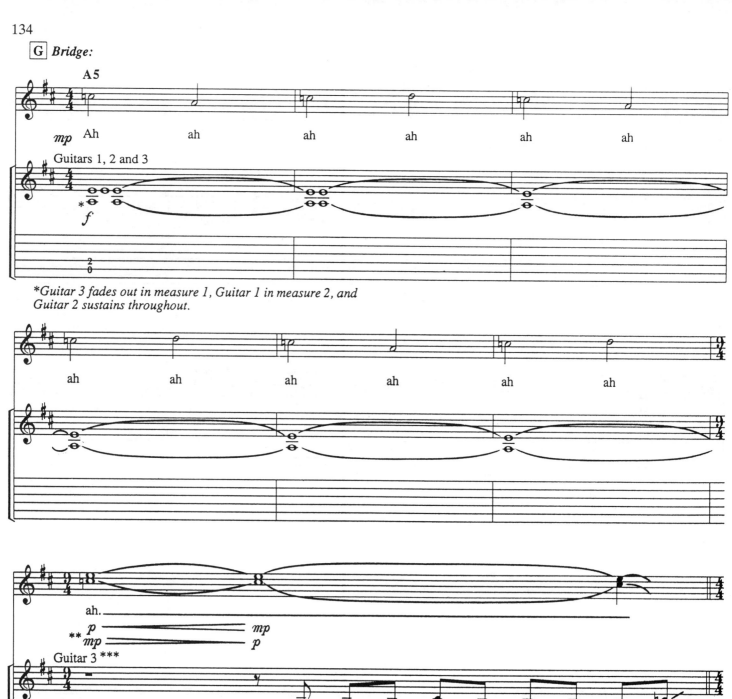

*Guitar 3 fades out in measure 1, Guitar 1 in measure 2, and
Guitar 2 sustains throughout.

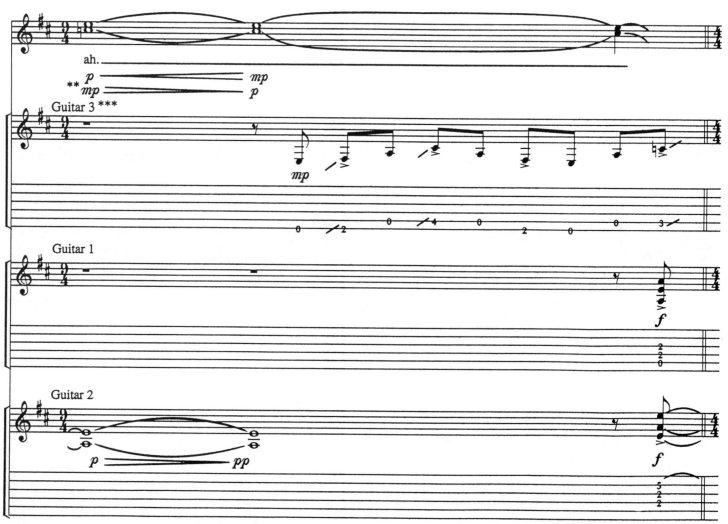

**Crescendo on upper note in vocal, decrescendo on the lower note.
***Guitar 3 is recorded through a Leslie amplifier (rotating speakers), and on a separate track with a standard amplifier.

R *Chorus 3(Guitar solo):*

Standard amplifier from here on, no Leslie.
**Volume in mix is much lower.*

Push it, ba - by, push it, ba - by, push it, ba - by,

push it, ba - by, push it, ba - by, push it, babe

Guitar 3

*Leslie amp returns, standard amp out.

Begin Guitar 4 figure 2
Guitar 4**

babe.

End Guitar 4 figure 2

**Guitar 1, figure 1 mixed lower to make room for Guitar 4, figure 1. (Right Channel)
Continue with Guitar 2, figure 1.

ooh, _____

Continue figure 1, Guitars 1 and 2 and continue figure 2, Guitar 4, 6 times till fade.

babe.

ooh, _____

aah _____ ooh.

ooh.
Let ring
Choke
I'd real - ly like to do it now.
Fade out
I'd real - ly like to do it now.

ROCK AND ROLL

Words and Music by
Jimmy Page, Robert Plant, John Paul Jones
and John Bonham

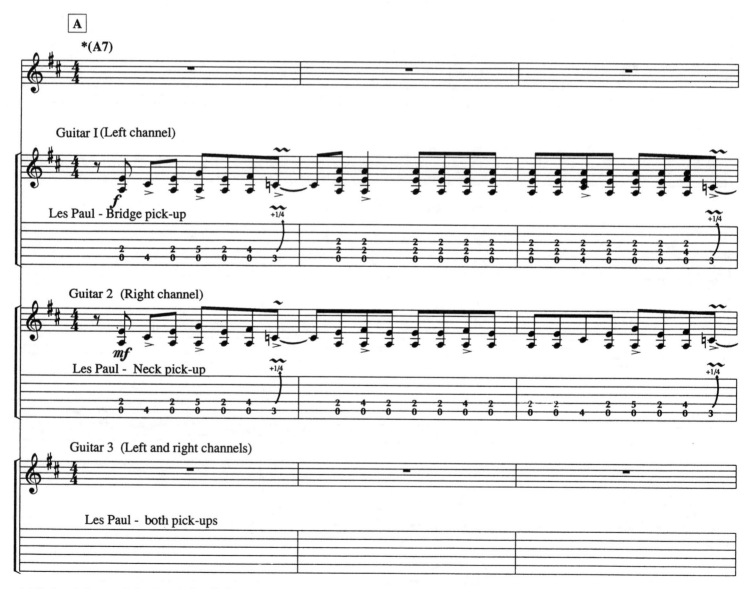

*All chords in parentheses are implied.

*Mute the sixth string with the fret hand thumb after bending G.

been a long time since I did the stroll. _____

Ooh, let me get it back, let me get it back, let me get it

back, ba - by where I ____ come from. ____

It's

*From here on Guitar I and II are written together. Guitars I and II continue to maintain their tones
(Guitar I: heavy distortion/ambient, Guitar II: light distortion/direct.)*

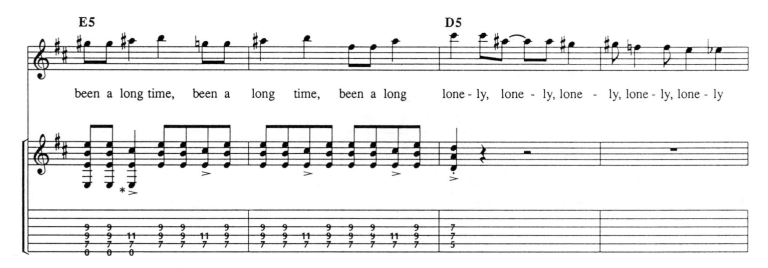

Let the sixth string ring.

E *Verse* *(Guitar Solo):*
(A7)

(D7)

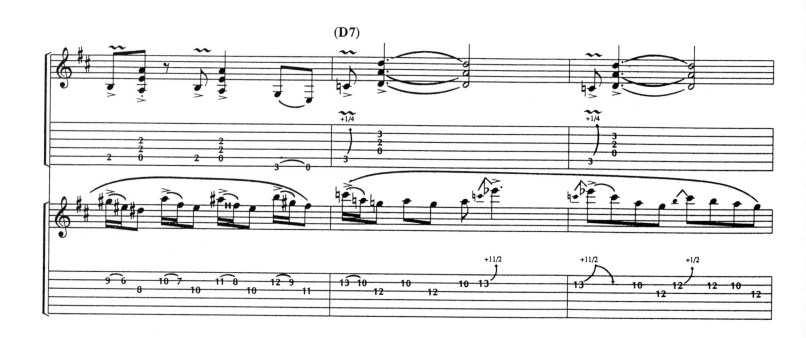

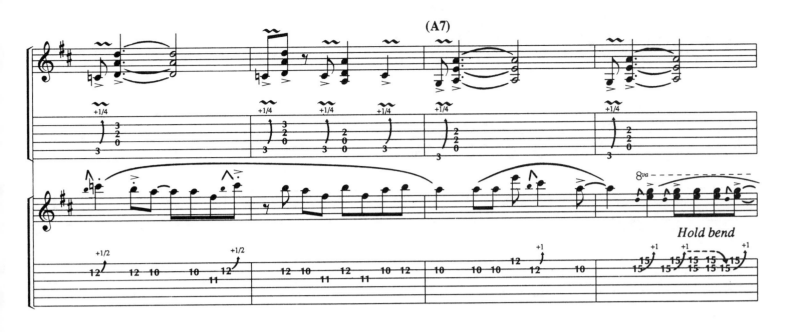

F Verse:
(A7)

Oh _____ it seems so long_ since we

Guitar 1

Guitar 3 out

walked in the moon - light._____ Mak- ing vows,_ that

just can't work right. ha- ha- yeah,_ Op- en your arms, op- en

(D7)

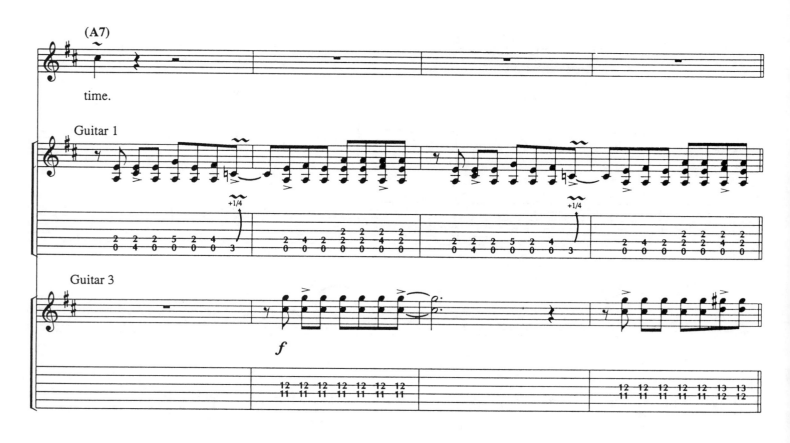

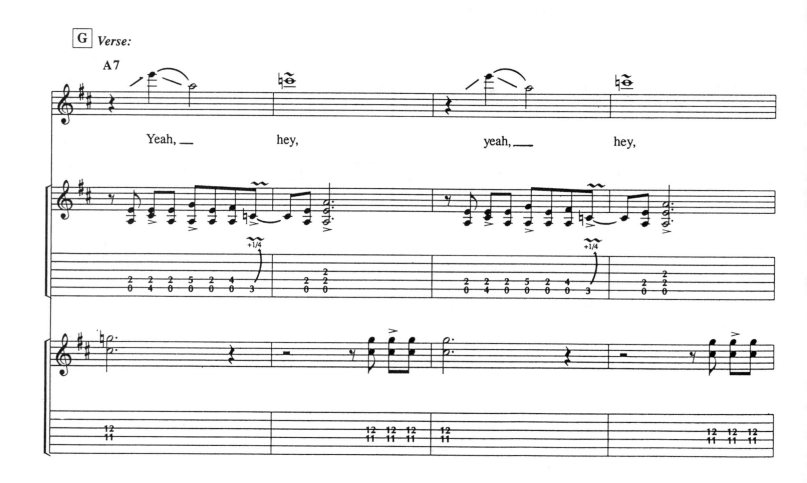

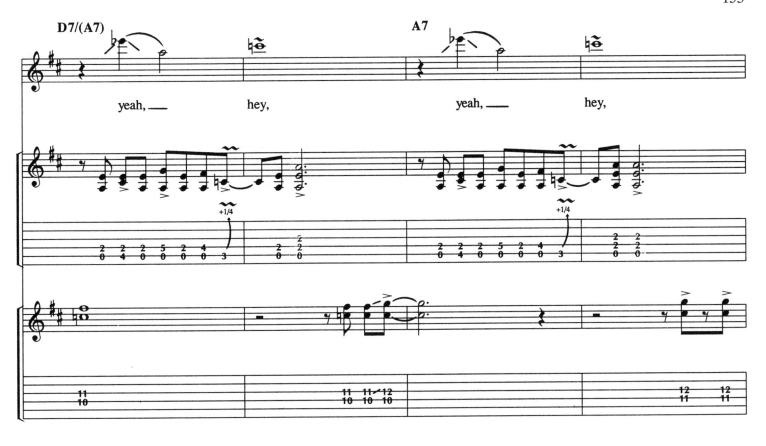

yeah, ___   hey,   yeah, ___   hey,

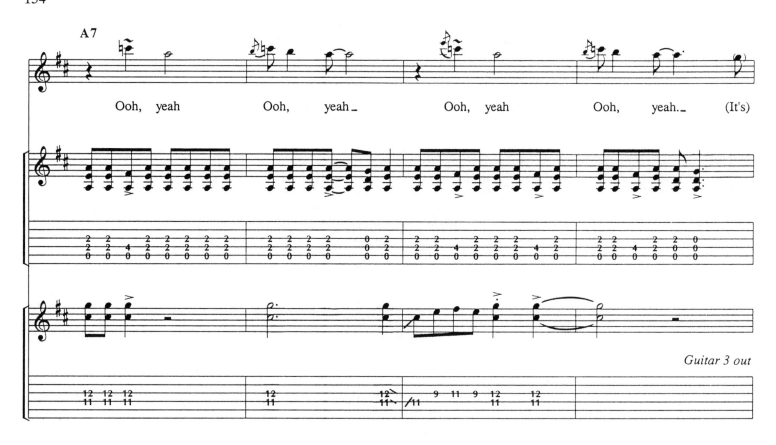

Drum Outro: *(free tempo)*

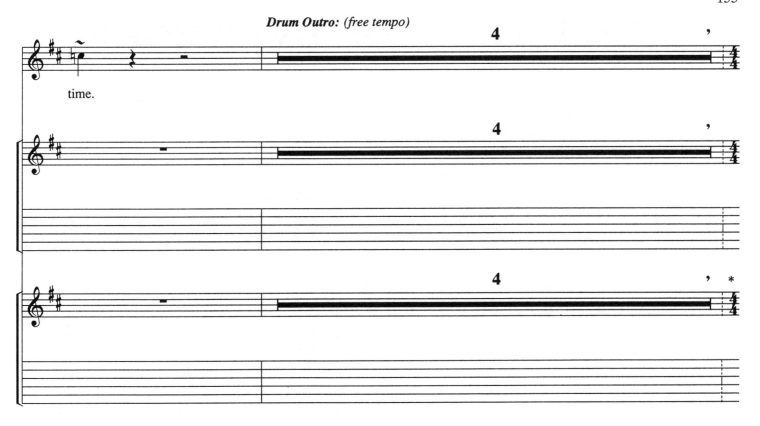

time.

On Cue

A7

Original tempo

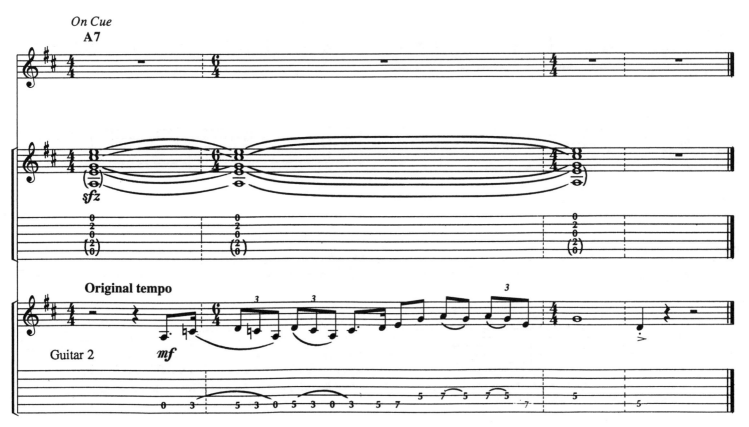

Guitar 2

Guitarist gives cue out of solo.

THE BATTLE OF EVERMORE

Words and Music by
Jimmy Page and Robert Plant

Mythical Folk Ballad freely   ♩ = 144
With a strong half-time feel

* *Composite of Mandolins 1 and 2.* ** *Arranged for Guitar with capo at X. All notes in TAB at X are notated as open.*
To be played one octave higher until **G**

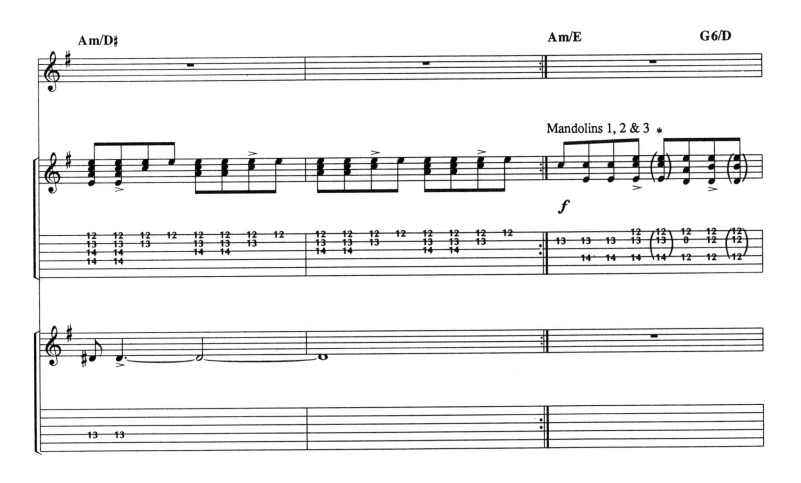

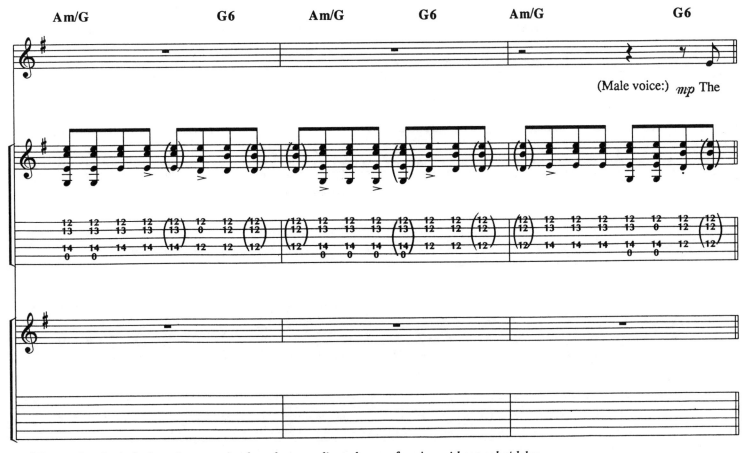

Tape echo. Include these beats to simulate the recording when performing without echo/delay.

B *Verse:*
Mandolins 1, 2 & 3

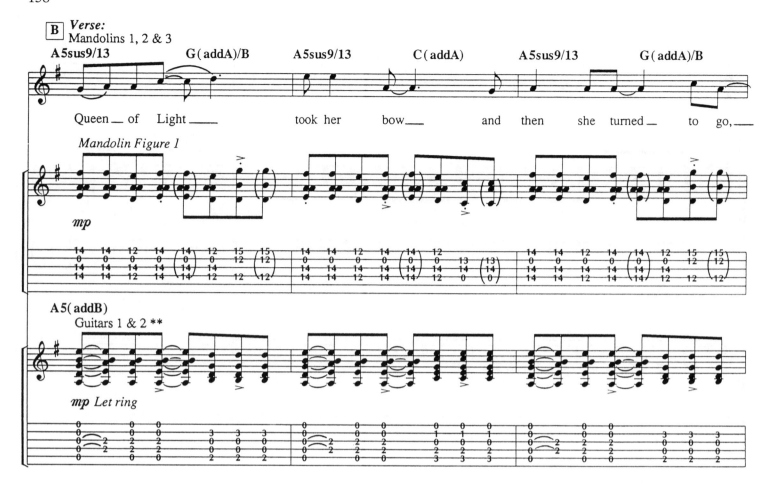

Queen — of Light ____ took her bow ____ and then she turned — to go, ____

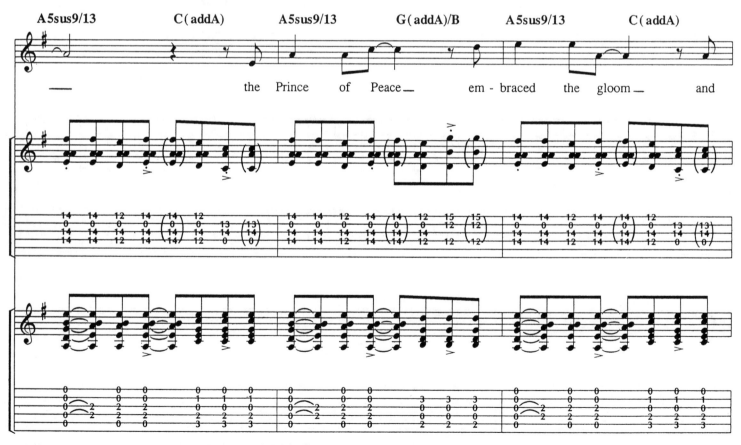

— the Prince of Peace — em - braced the gloom — and

* *Chord names are a composite of the Mandolin & Guitar parts.*

** *Six and Twelve string Guitars.*

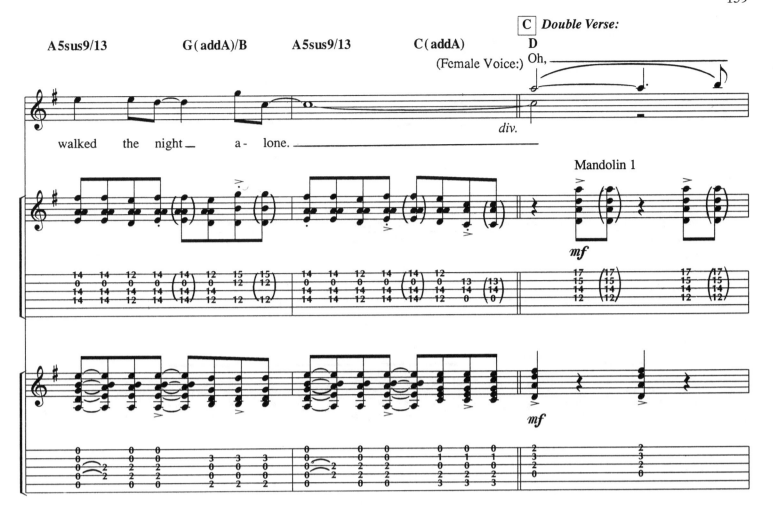

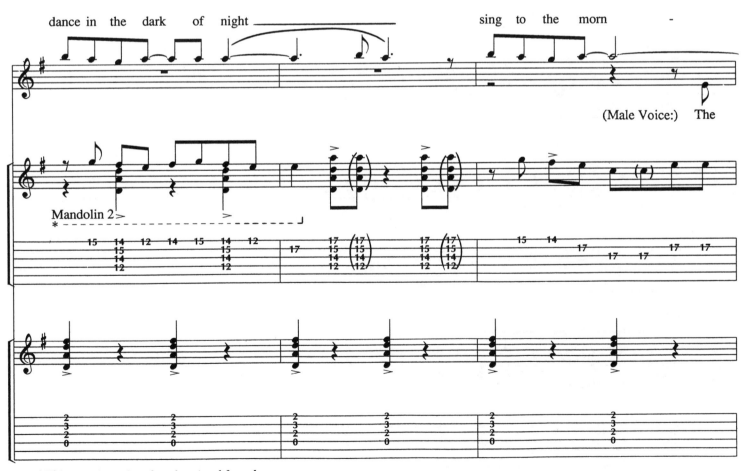

This part is optional and omitted from here on.

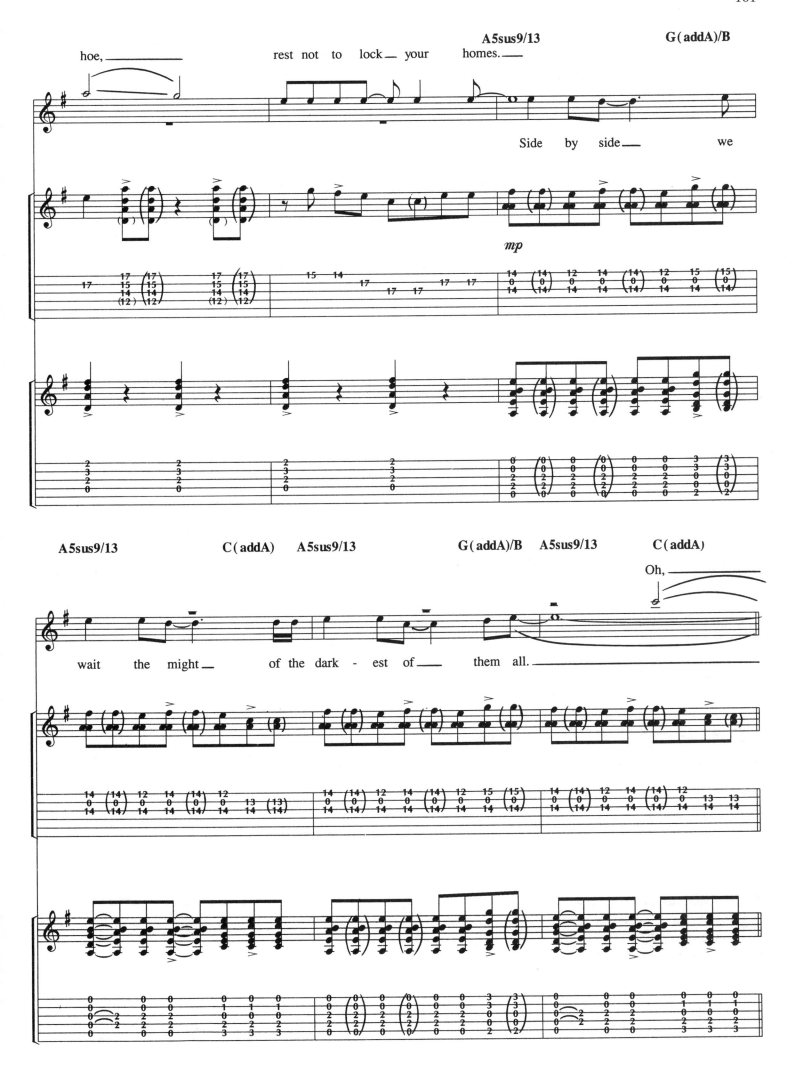

E   D

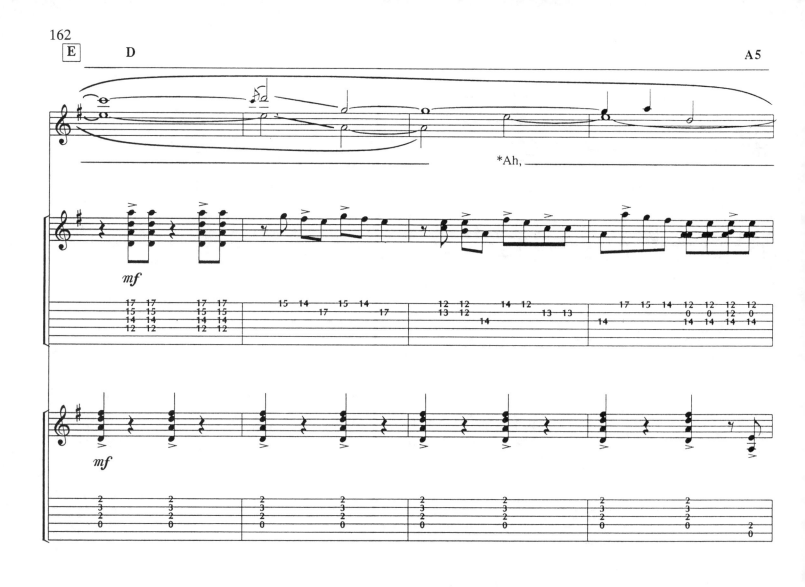

*Ah,

A5sus9/13   G(addA)   A5sus9/13   C(addA)   A5sus9/13   G(addA)

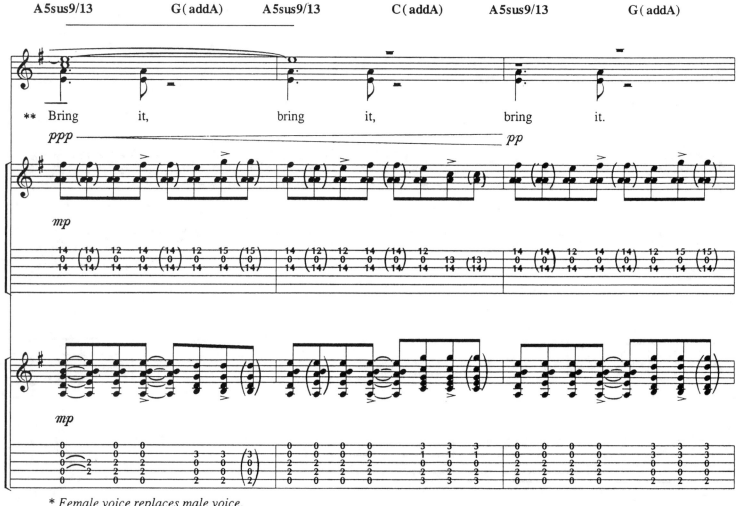

** Bring   it,   bring   it,   bring   it.

*Female voice replaces male voice.
**Distant Male Chorus. (Right Channel)

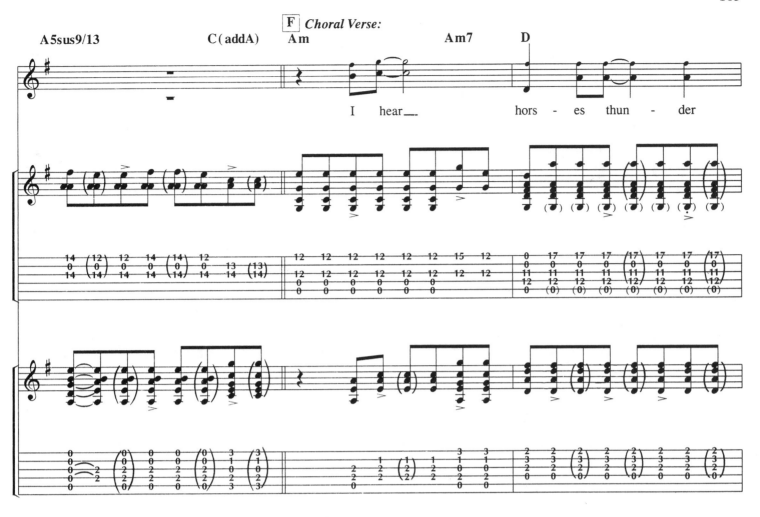

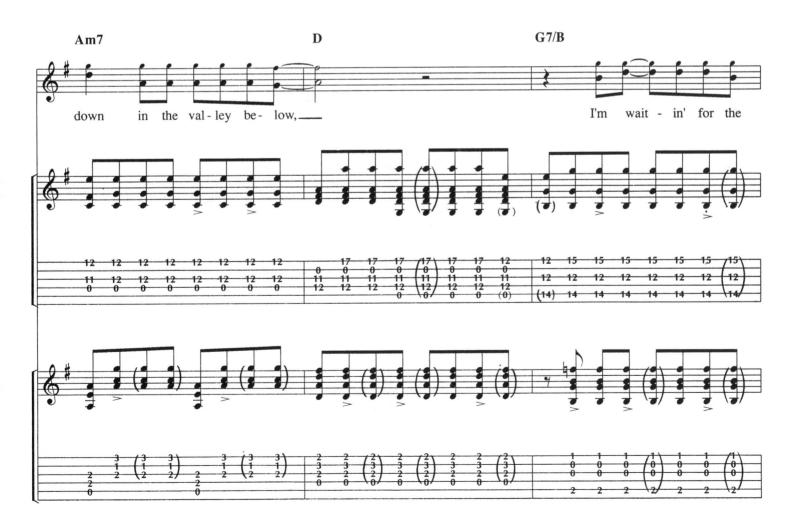

From here on the Guitar arrangement is notated without the tape echo rhythms.

* Female voice replaces male voice.

P *Choral Verse:*

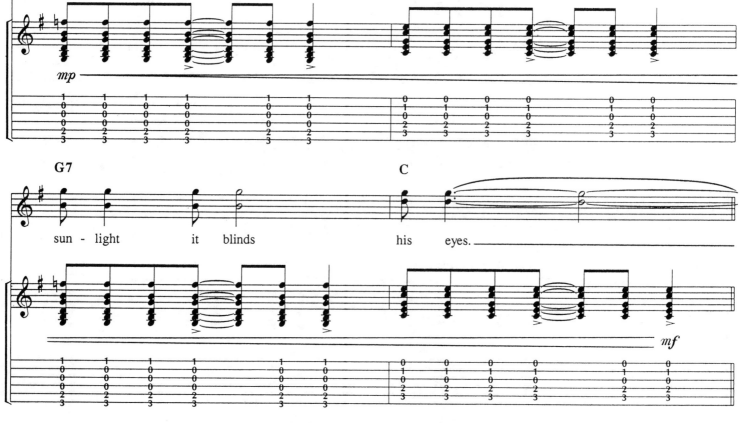

At last, ____ the sun ____ is shin - in' the ____ clouds ____ of blue ____ roll by. ____ With flames ____ from the dra - gon of dark - ness the sun - light it blinds his eyes. ____

* Long crescendo next 24 bars to forte.

*The suggested strum is intended to emphasize the descending line of the mandolin within a counterrhythm. When playing with the recording, be careful with the tempo.
** Play fingerstyle. The low nòtes are strummed with the thumb or pick and the high notes are plucked with the fingers.

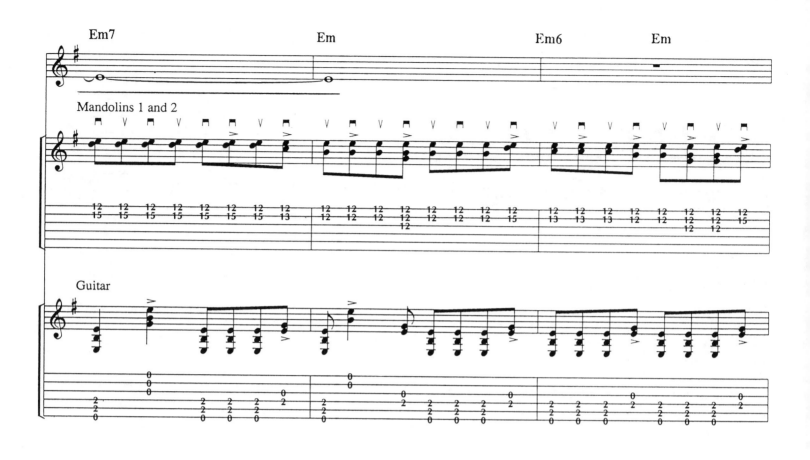

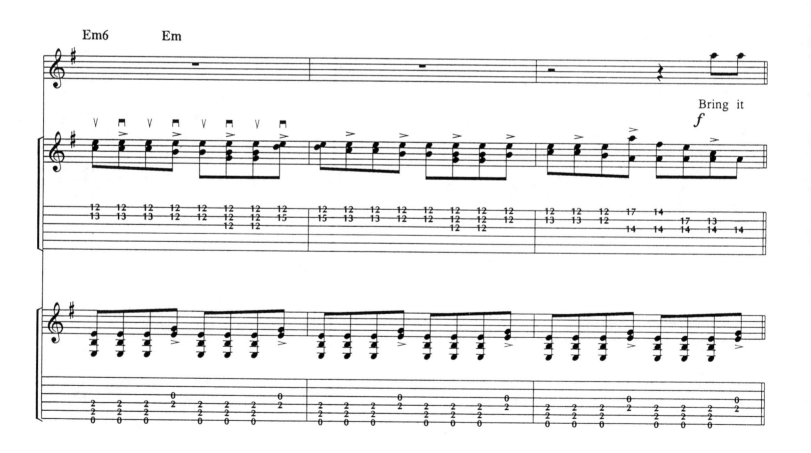

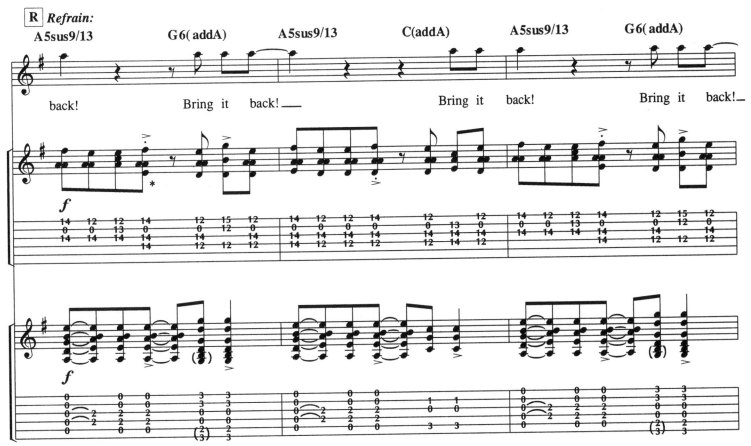

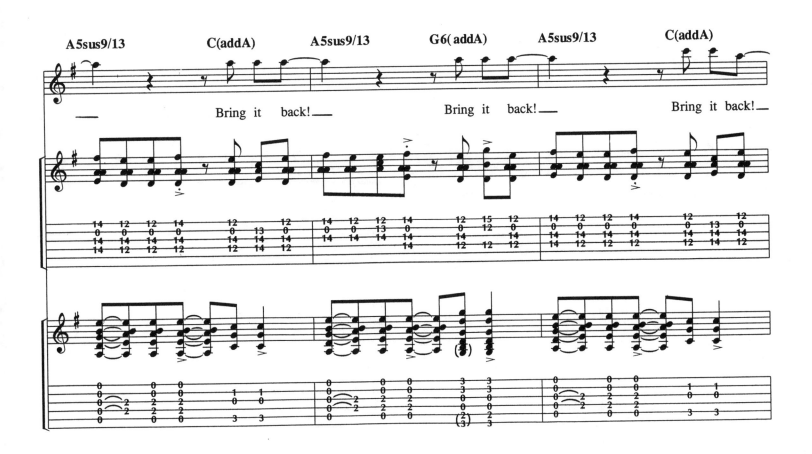

* Due to fingering difficulties, all notes on ④ and ⑤ are optional.

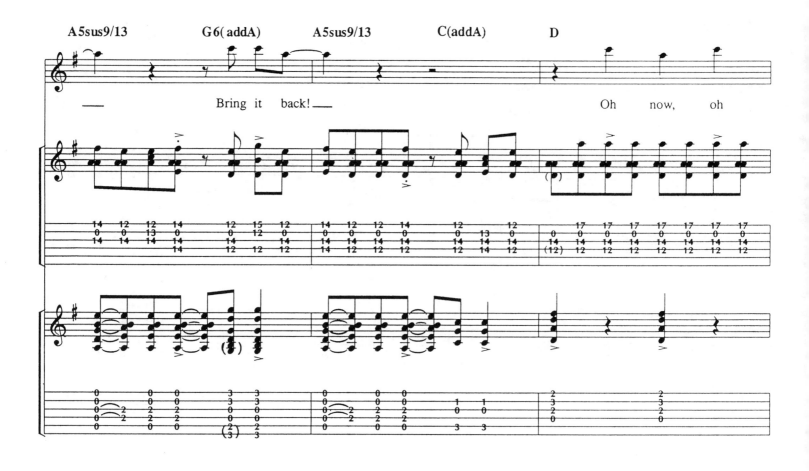

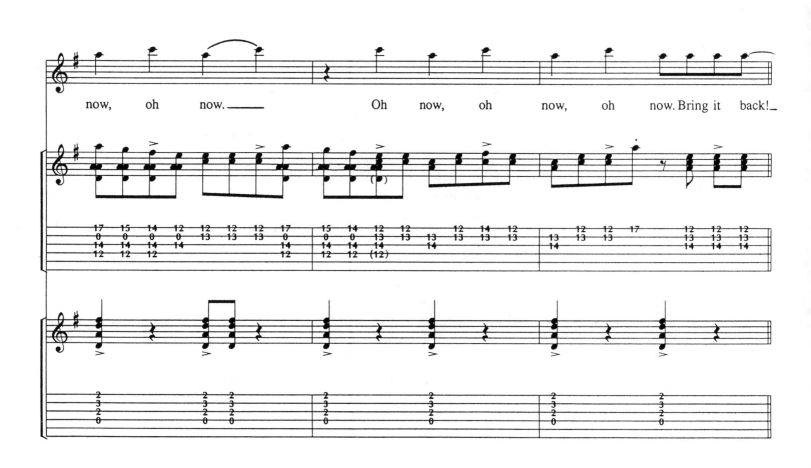

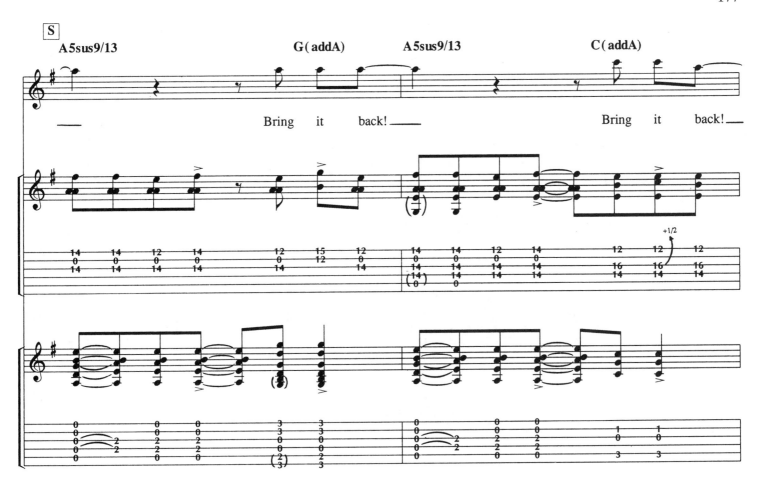

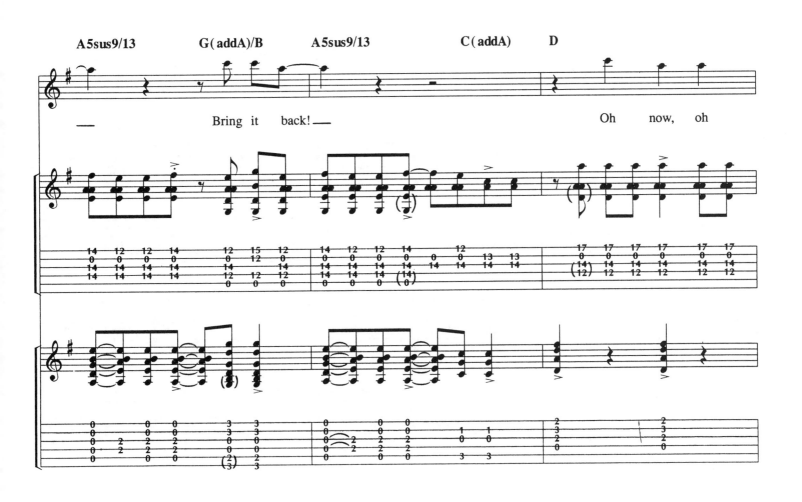

now oh now oh.   Oh now, oh now, oh now. Bring it!

T *Coda:*

A5sus9/13   G(addA)   A5sus9/13   C(addA)

Bring it!   Bring it!   Bring it!   Bring it! ____ Bring it!

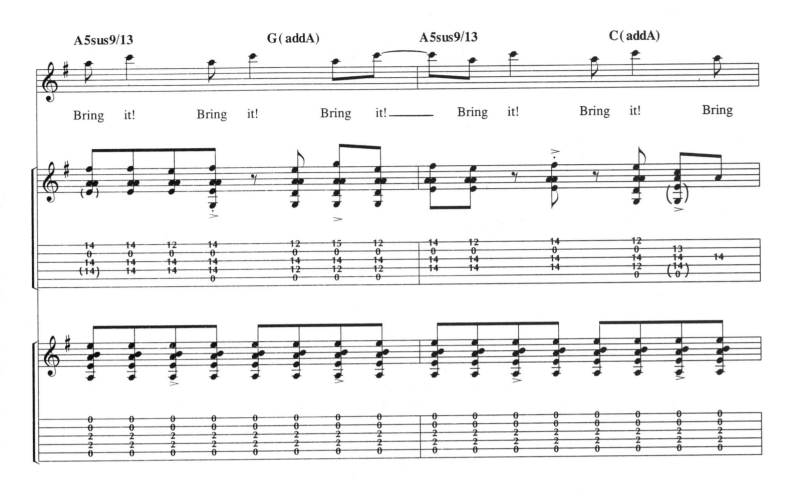

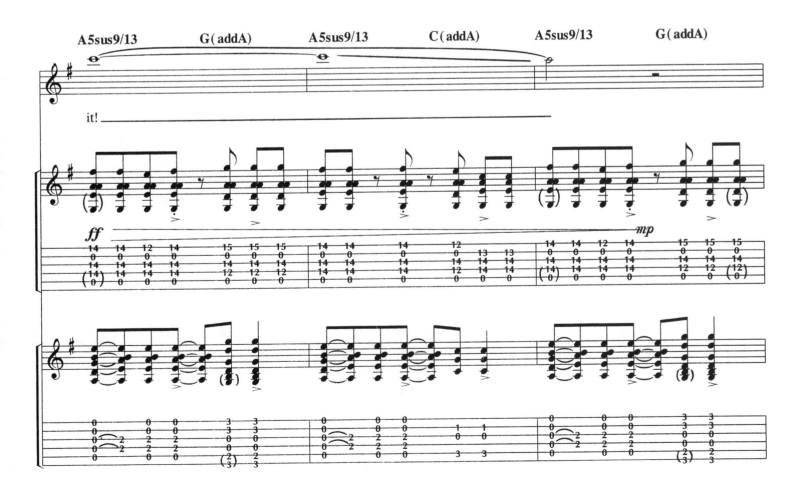

WHEN THE LEVEE BREAKS

Words and Music by
Jimmy Page, Robert Plant, John Paul Jones,
John Bonham and Memphis Minnie

*Bb major or an F Blues harp.

**Open F tuning: ④ = C, ③ = F, ② = A, ① = C. ⑥ and ⑤ aren't used in the recording.
12 string octave and unison strings aren't notated. Slide is worn on fourth finger to be ready for [A].

***Implied.

Guitars 1 appear with phase shifting until the following verse.
*Worn on fourth finger.

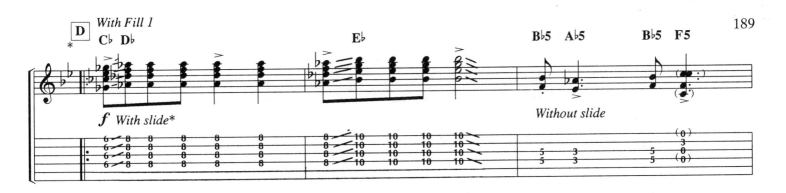

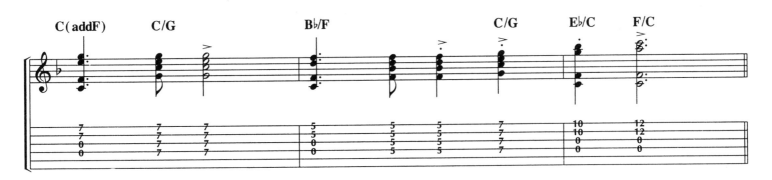

*Guitar 1 appears with phase shifting for the rest of the song.

**These chord names are implied by the guitar only and do not reflect the bass part.

***A Les Paul in standard tuning through a fuzztone and played with a slide.

make ya' feel bad___ when ya' tryin' ta' find your way home ya' don't know___ which way (to) go,___

Let ring

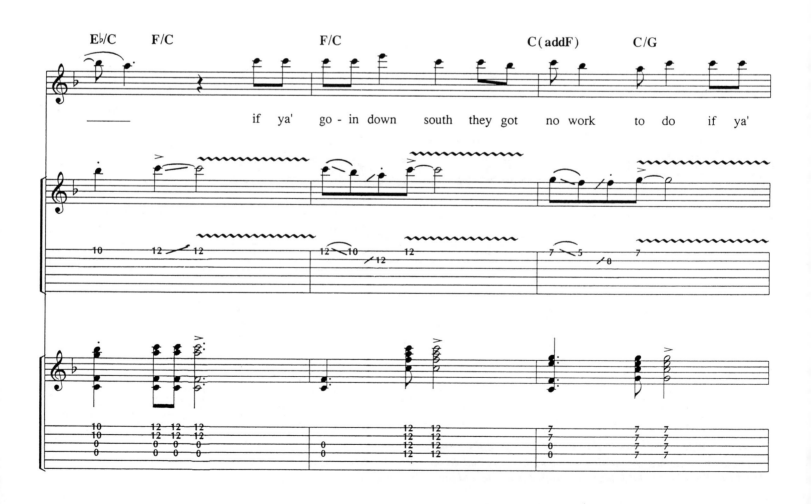

___ if ya' go - in down south they got no work to do if ya'

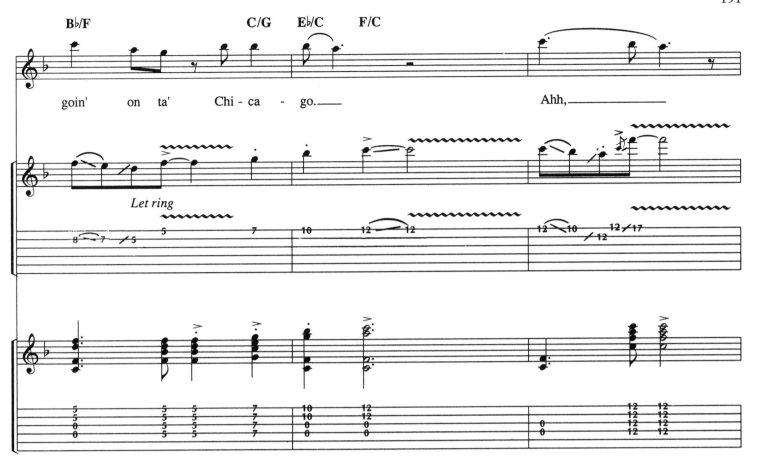

goin' on ta' Chi - ca - go.＿＿＿ Ahh,＿＿＿＿＿＿＿

Let ring

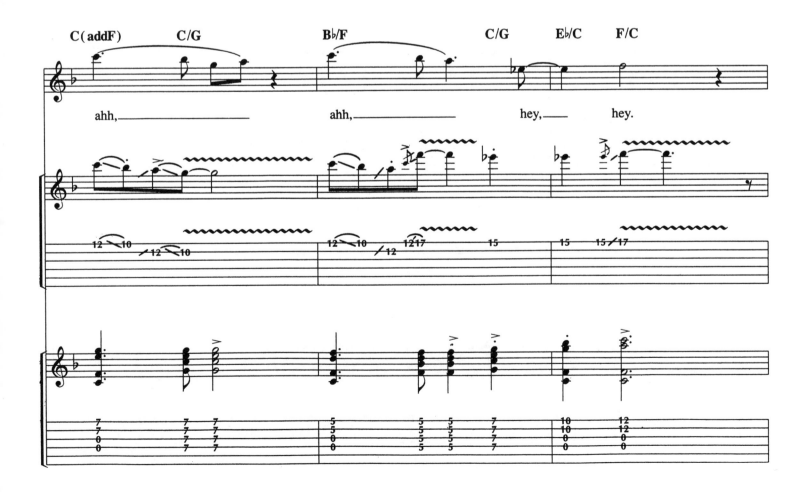

ahh,＿＿＿＿＿＿＿ ahh,＿＿＿＿＿ hey,＿ hey.

*Final note of phrase from Guitar 2.

With Guitar 2 Rhythm Figure 1
With ad lib. variations

*Arpeggiate.
**Harmonica first time only.

Blues Harp first time only.
**Guitars 1 & 2 are combined.*

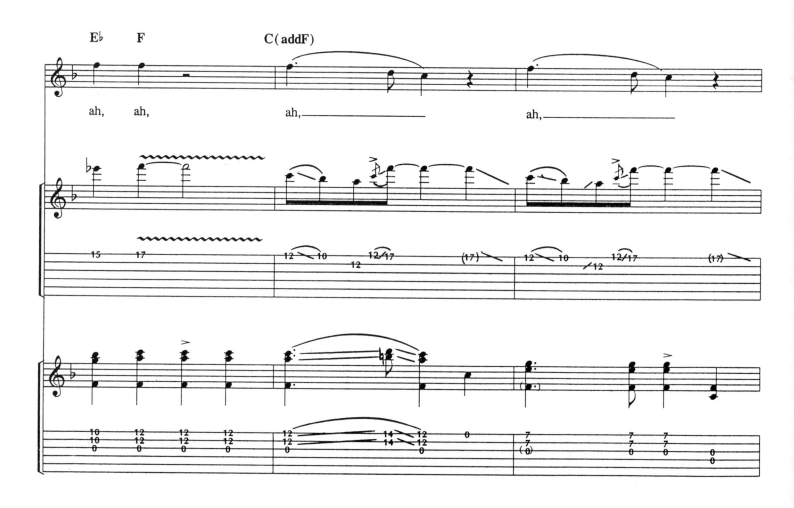

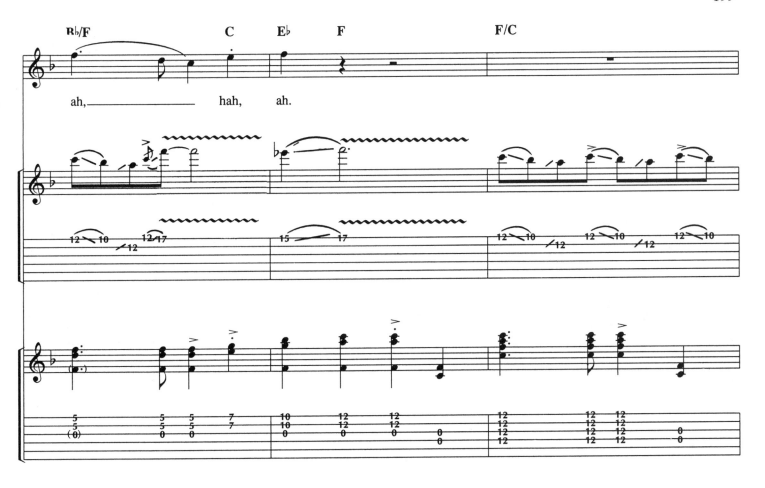

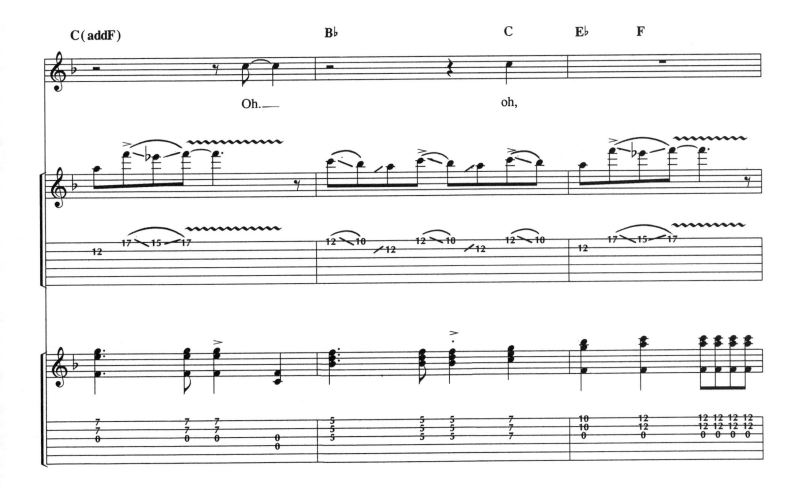

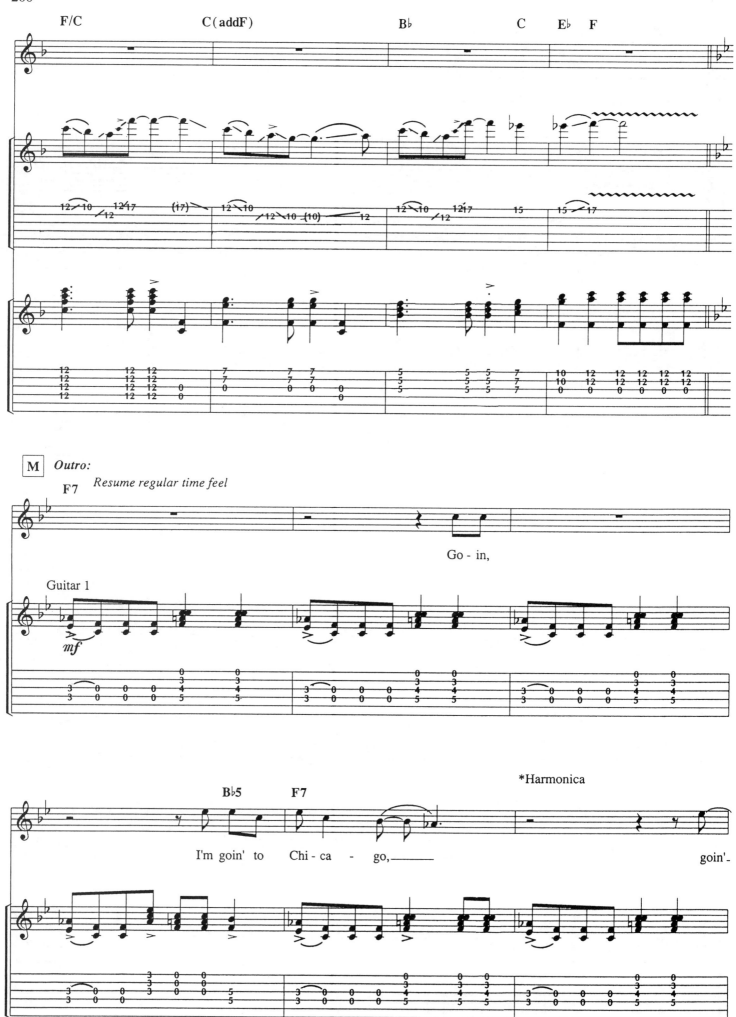

Harmonica with backwards echo enters and continues intermittently for the remainder of the song.

Guitar 1 gradually panned to the left.
**Guitar 1 gradually panned right.*

*Slide Guitar (backwards echo track only).
**Panned left and right every four measures.

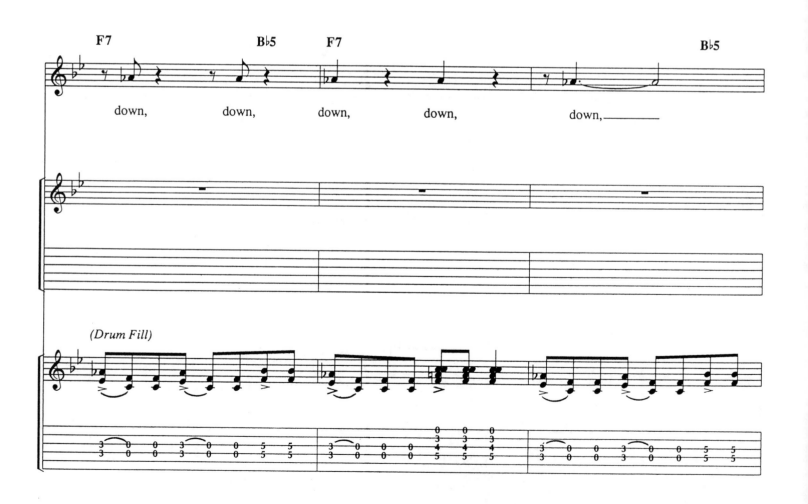

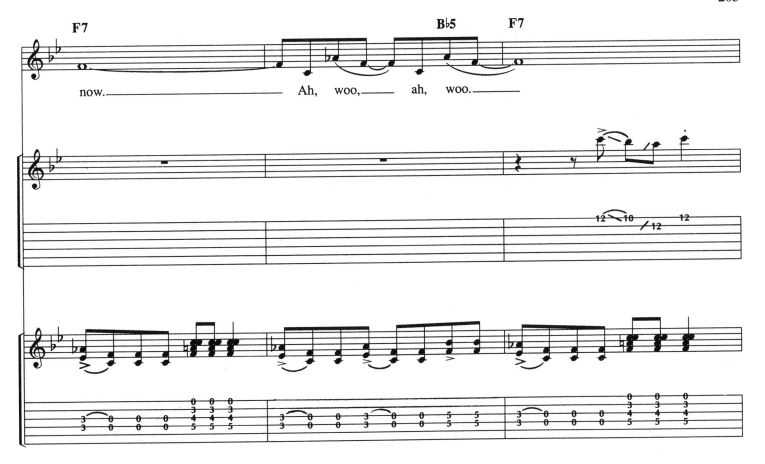

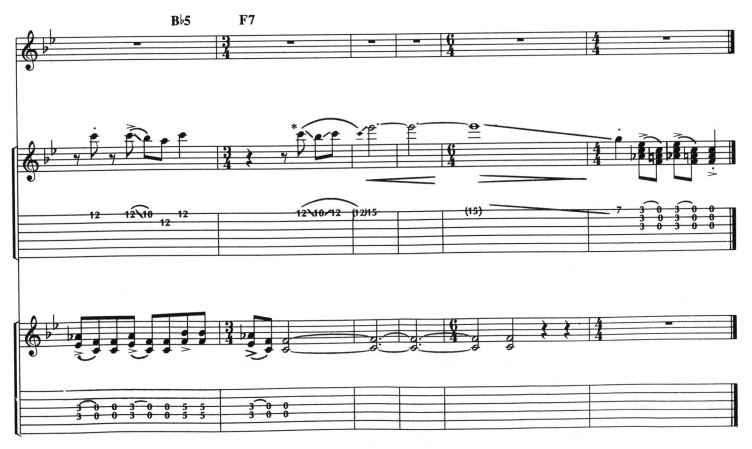

Backwards echo track only from here on.
The notation and techniques are an approximation of the original recording.

STAIRWAY TO HEAVEN

Epical Ballad: Chamber Folk to Heavy Rock
Slowly ♩ = 72 *(gradual accellerando)*

Words and Music by
Jimmy Page and Robert Plant

Capo at VII using a cutaway guitar with easy access to the 22nd fret. All notes in TAB at VII are open strings.

**The open first string is not played here, but rings sympathetically.*

***A gradual decrescendo continues for the next four measures to allow for the entrance of the recorders.*

*The actual pitch of this note(e) is one octave higher

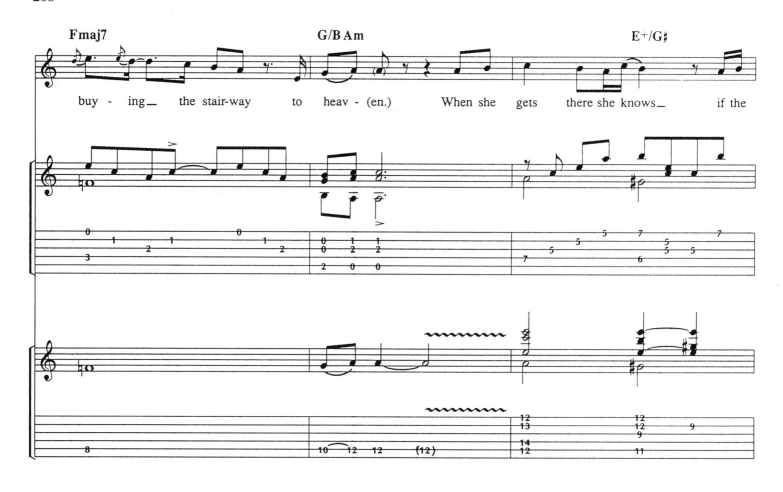

buy - ing___ the stair-way to heav - (en.) When she gets there she knows___ if the

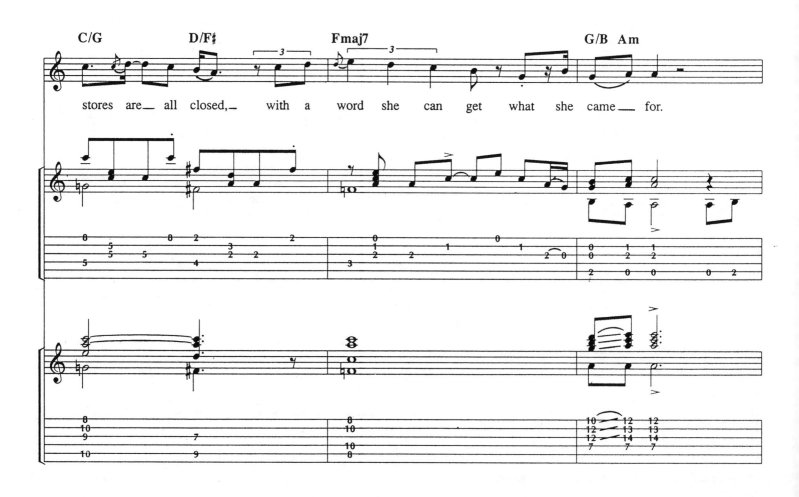

stores are___ all closed,___ with a word she can get what she came___ for.

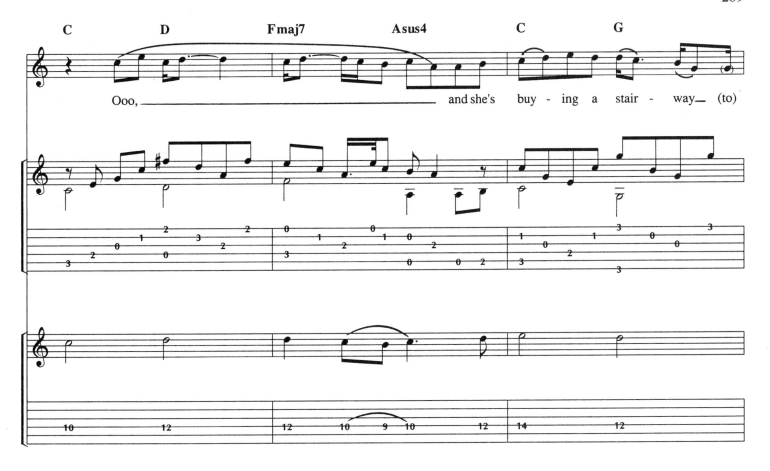

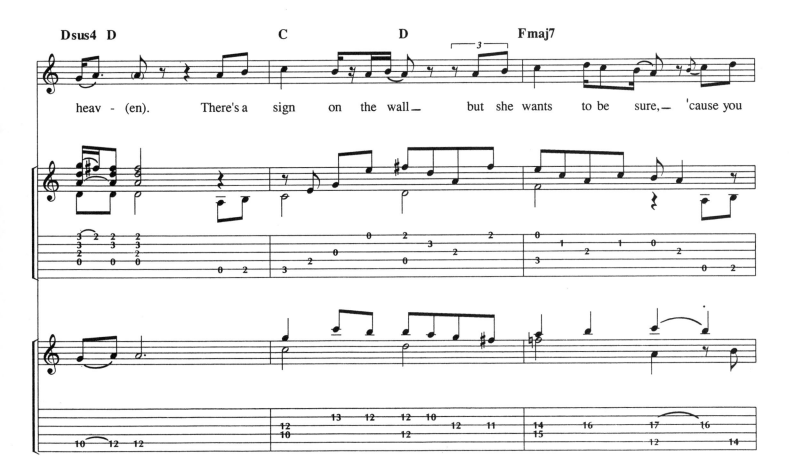

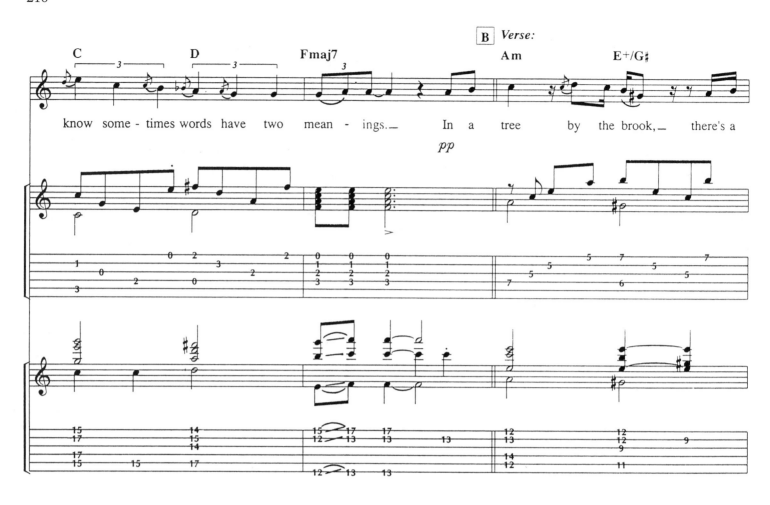

know some-times words have two mean-ings.— In a tree by the brook,— there's a

pp

song-bird— who sings,— some-times all of our thoughts are mis - giv - en.

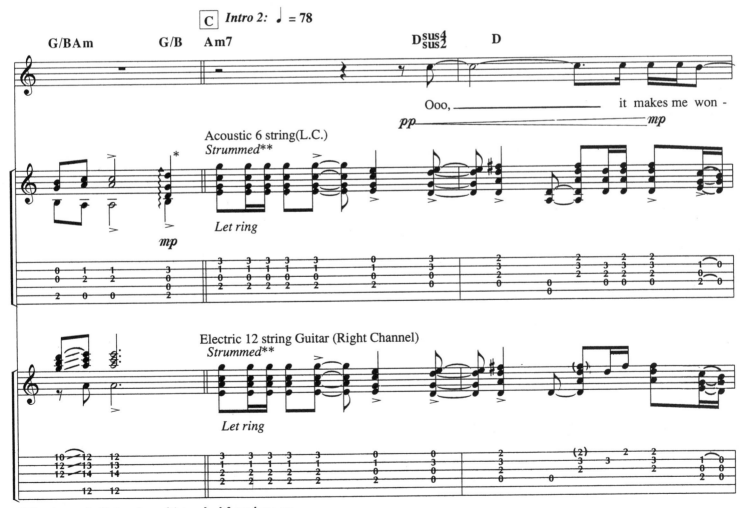

The Acoustic Guitar is multi-tracked from here on.
**With a pick.*

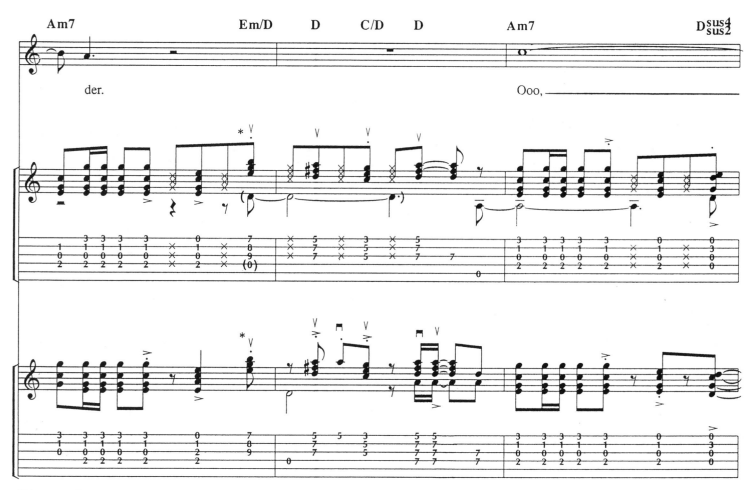

*Suggested strum

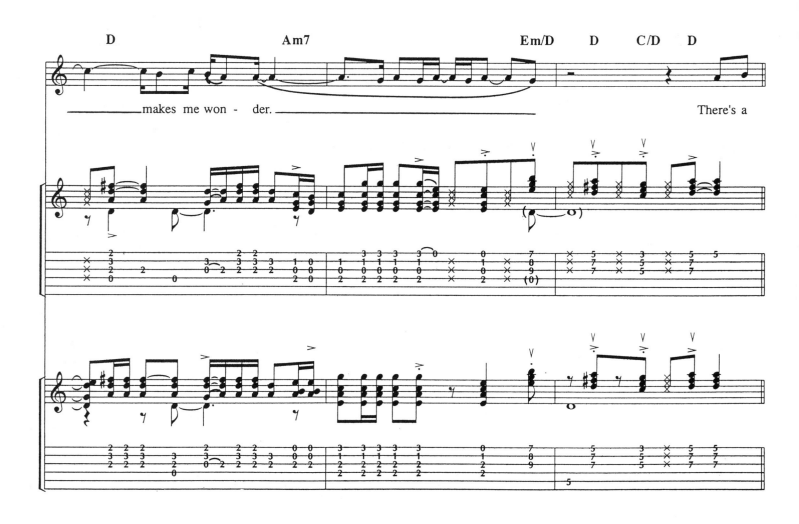

*Suggested fingering.

**T=Thumb on ⑥

voic - es of those who stand look - ing.

Acoustic 6 string

Electric 12 string 1

Electric 12 string 2 (R&LC)   *Rhythm Figure 2*

Ooo, _____ it makes me won - der.

pp cresc.

mp

End Rhythm Figure 2   *Gtr. 2 Tacet*

* Strings ④ and ② are muted while ③ and ① are open.

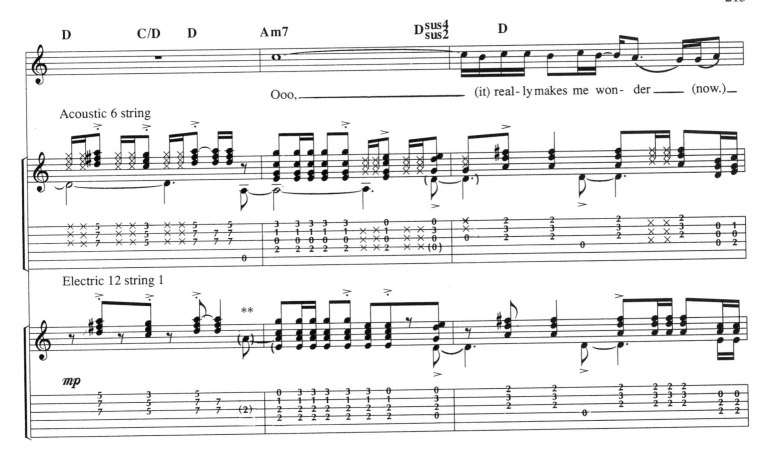

Ooo,_____ (it) real- ly makes me won- der _____ (now.)_

Acoustic 6 string

Electric 12 string 1

mp

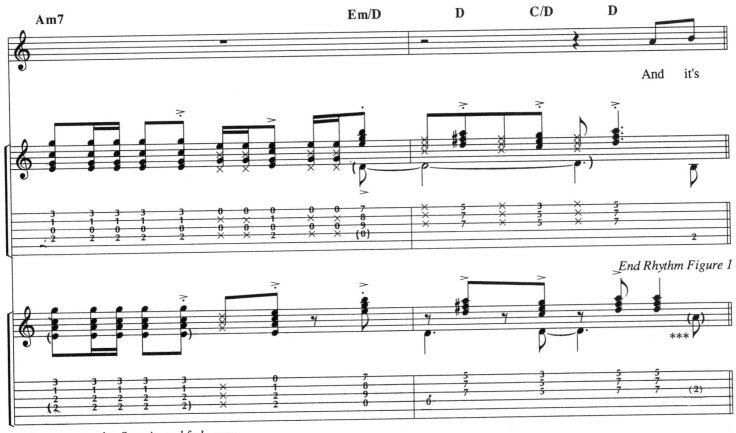

And it's

End Rhythm Figure 1

**Separate track – Sustain and fade over.*

***Separate track.*

E *Verse:* *With Rhythm Figure 1 (Electric 12 string) with ad lib variations.*

Whis - pered that soon— if we all— call— the tune,— then the pi - per will lead us to reas-

on. And a new day— will dawn,— for those who stand long,— and the

With Rhythm Figure 2 (Electric 12 string)

for - ests will ech - o with laugh - ter.

Oh. _____

F *Verse:* *With Rhythm Figure 1*
♩ = 90 *With ad lib variations.*

(Drums enter)

If there's a bust-le in your

hedge-row, don't be a-larmed now, it's just a spring clean for the May queen.

Yes there are two paths you can go by, but in the long run, there's still time to change the road

*Doubled with an Electric 6 string (Telecaster?) from here on.

**( ) Acoustic Guitar track only.

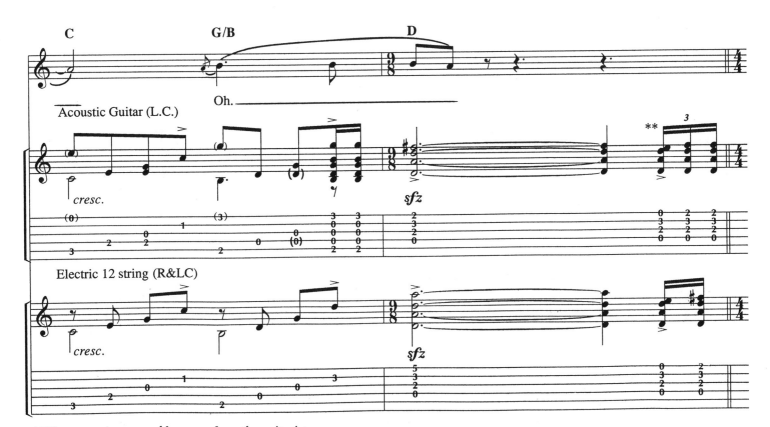

**The tempo is resumed by a cue from the guitarist.*

*Notes in parenthesis are upper notes of quieter background track.

*1958 Telecaster through a Fender Suproamp?

** punch in from a separate track

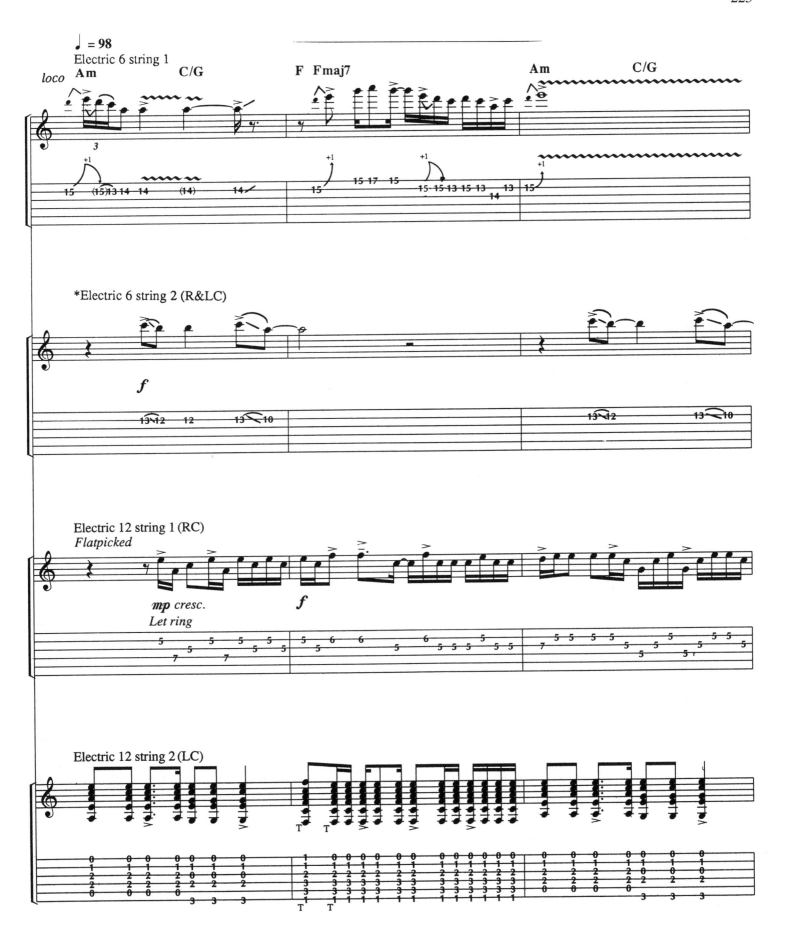

*Played with a glass or metal slide.

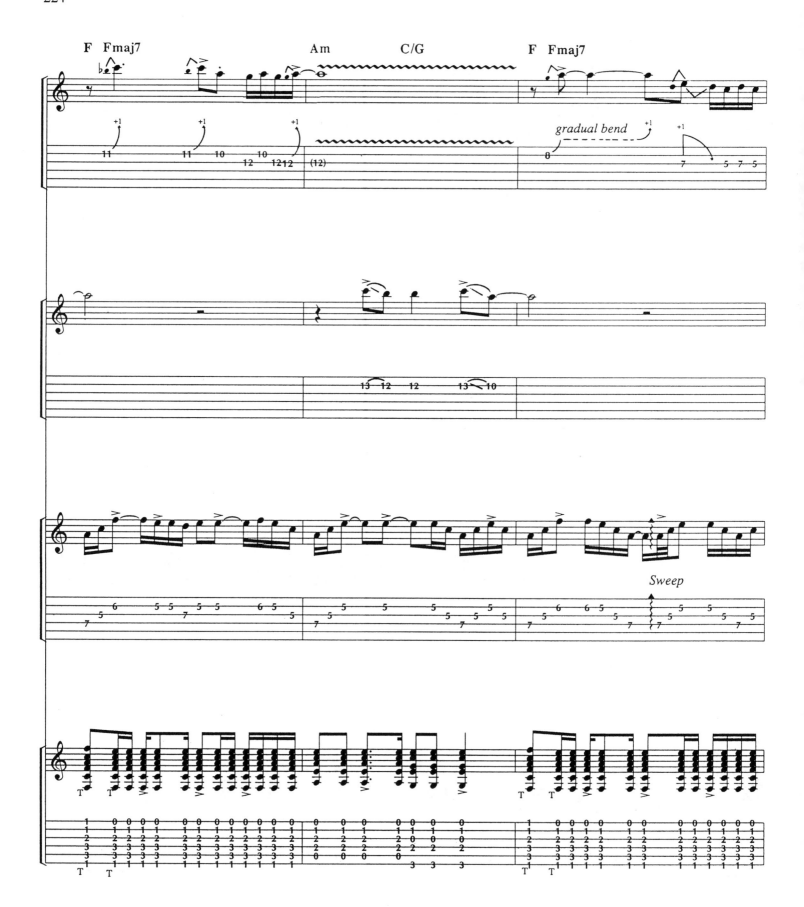

J *Verse:* *With Rhythm Figure 3 with ad lib variations*

♩ = **102**

*Palm muting is alternated (off then on) as in this two measure phrase from here on, but not notated.

Rhythm Figure 3
Electric 12 string Guitar 3 (RC)

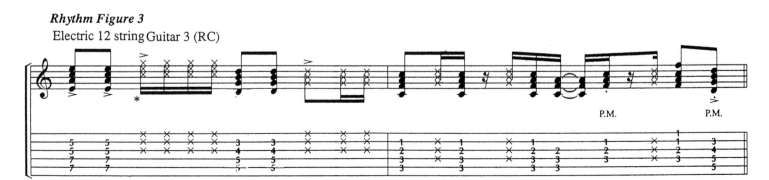

*Mute strings with fret hand at current chord position.

Right and left channels from here on.

228

gold._____ And if you list-en ver-y hard,_____

*Pan to center.

**Doubling ends.

Lead vocal in downstems, distorted chorus track in upstems.

*Pre-bent from here on

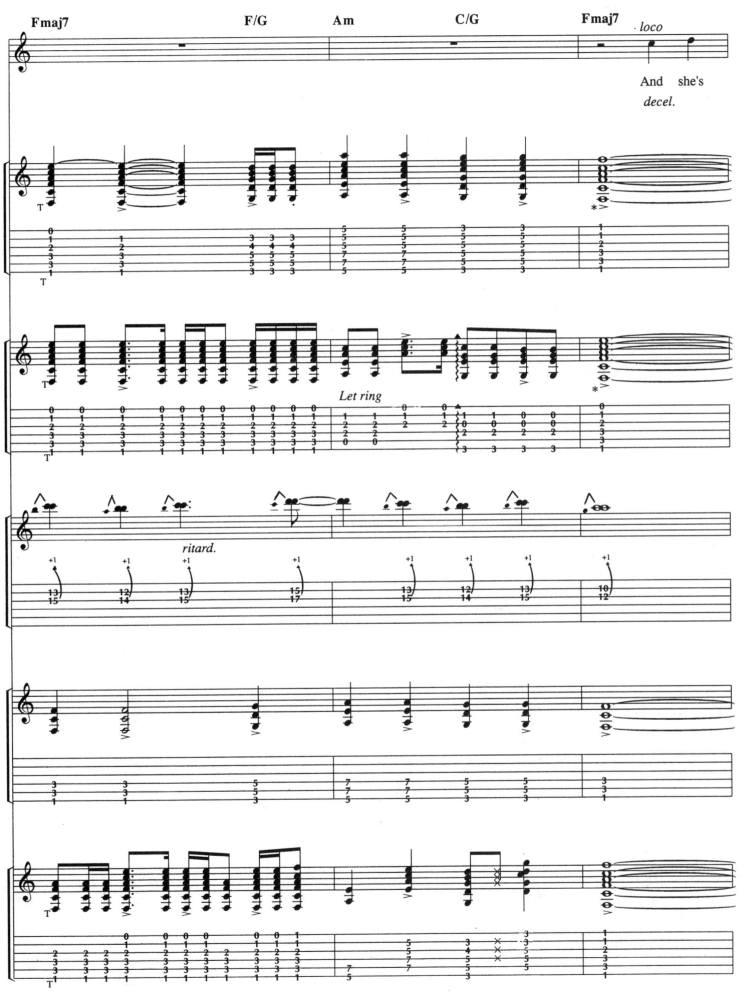

And she's

*VSO (variable speed/pitch oscilator) 1/2 step glide.

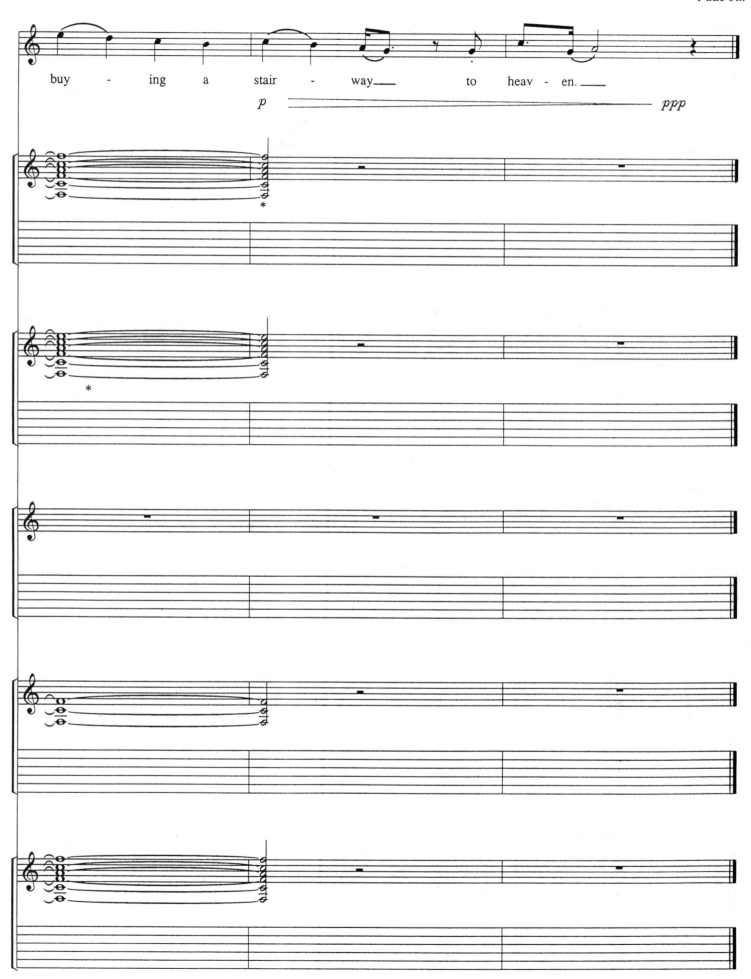

Fade out

buy - ing a stair - way___ to heav - en. ___

p ———————————————————————— *ppp*

Oscillate guitar volume knob rhythmically.

Notation and Tablature Explained

Open C chord

Scale of E major

High E (1st) string
B (2nd) string
G (3rd) string
D (4th) string
A (5th) string
Low E (6th) string

Bent Notes

The note fretted is always shown first. Variations in pitch achieved by string bending are enclosed within this symbol ⌐ ⌐. If you aren't sure how far to bend the string, playing the notes indicated without bending gives a guide to the pitches to aim for. The following examples cover the most common string bending techniques:

Example 1
Play the D, bend up one tone (two half-steps) to E.

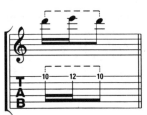

Example 2
Play the D, bend up one tone to E then release bend to sound D. Only the first note is picked.

Example 3
Fast bend: Play the D, then bend up one tone to E as quickly as possible.

Example 4
Pre-bend: fret the D, bend up one tone to E, then pick.

Example 5
Play the A and D together, then bend the B-string up one tone to sound B.

Example 6
Play the D and F♯ together, then bend the G-string up one tone to E, and the B-string up a semitone to G.

Additional guitaristic techniques have been notated as follows:

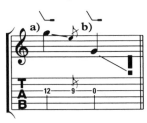

Tremolo Bar
Alter pitch using tremolo bar. Where possible, the pitch to aim for is shown.
a) Play the G; use the bar to drop the pitch to E.
b) Play the open G; use the bar to 'divebomb', i.e. drop the pitch as far as possible.

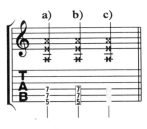

Mutes
a) Right hand mute
Mute strings by resting the right hand on the strings just above the bridge.
b) Left hand mute
Damp the strings by releasing left hand pressure just after the notes sound.
c) Unpitched mute
Damp the strings with the left hand to produce a percussive sound.

Hammer on and Pull off
Play first note, sound next note by 'hammering on', the next by 'pulling off'. Only the first note is picked.

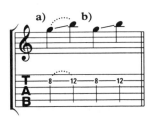

Glissando
a) Play first note, sound next note by sliding up string. Only the first note is picked.
b) As above, but pick second note.

Natural Harmonics
Touch the string over the fret marked, and pick to produce a bell-like tone. The small notes show the resultant pitch, where necessary.

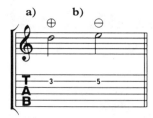

Slide Guitar
a) Play using slide.
b) Play without slide.

Artificial Harmonics
Fret the lowest note, touch string over fret indicated by diamond notehead and pick. Small notes show the resultant pitch.

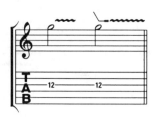

Vibrato
Apply vibrato, by 'shaking' note or with tremolo bar. As vibrato is so much a matter of personal taste and technique, it is indicated only where essential.

Pinch Harmonics
Fret the note as usual, but 'pinch' or 'squeeze' the string with the picking hand to produce a harmonic overtone. Small notes show the resultant pitch.

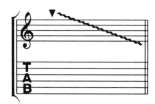

Pick Scratch
Scrape the pick down the strings – this works best on the wound strings.

Microtones
A downwards arrow means the written pitch is lowered by less than a semitone; an upwards arrow raises the written pitch.

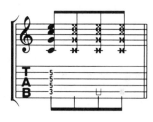

Repeated Chords
To make rhythm guitar parts easier to read the tablature numbers may be omitted when a chord is repeated. The example shows a C major chord played naturally, r/h muted, l/h muted and as an unpitched mute respectively.

Special Tunings
Non-standard tunings are shown as 'tuning boxes'. Each box represents one guitar string, the leftmost box corresponding to the lowest pitched string. The symbol '•' in a box means the pitch of the corresponding string is not altered. A note within a box means the string must be re-tuned as stated. For tablature readers, numbers appear in the boxes. The numbers represent the number of half-steps the string must be tuned up or down. The tablature relates to an instrument tuned as stated.

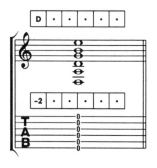

Tune the low E (6th) string down one tone (two half-steps) to D.

Chord naming
The following chord naming convention has been used:

Where there is no appropriate chord box, for example when the music consists of a repeated figure (or riff) the tonal base is indicated in parenthesis: [C]

Where it was not possible to transcribe a passage, the symbol $\sim$ appears.

Indications sur la notation musicale et les tablatures

Accord de Do majeur ouvert

Gamme de Mi majeur

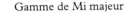

Mi aigu: 1ère corde
Si: 2e corde
Sol: 3e corde
Ré: 4e corde
La: 5e corde
Mi grave: 6e corde

Bending

La note correspondant à la case sur laquelle on pose le doigt est toujours indiquée en premier. Les variations de hauteur sont obienues en poussant sur la corde et sont indiquées par le symbole: ⌐ ⌐. En cas de doute sur la hauteur à atteindre, le fait de jouer les notes indiquées sans pousser sur la corde permet de trouver ensuite la bonne hauteur. Les examples suivants démontrent les techniques de bending les plus courantes.

Exemple 1
Jouez la note Ré et poussez la corde d'un ton (deux demi-tons) pour atteindre le Mi.

Exemple 2
Jouez le Ré, poussez sur la corde pour atteindre le Mi un ton plus haut, relâchez ensuite pour revenir au Ré. Seule la première note est jouée avec le médiator.

Exemple 3
'Fast Bend': jouez le Ré et poussez le plus rapidement possible pour atteindre le Mi.

Exemple 4
'Pre-bend': posez le doigt sur la case de Ré, poussez d'un ton pour atteindre le Mi avant de jouer la note.

Exemple 5
Jouez La et Ré simultanément; poussez ensuite sur la corde de Si pour atteindre la note Si.

Exemple 6
Jouez Ré et Fa♯ simultanément; poussez la corde de Sol d'un ton vers le Mi, et la corde de Si d'un demi-ton vers le Sol.

D'autres techniques de guitare sont notées de la façon suivante:

Emploi du levier de vibrato
Modifiez la hauteur du son avec le levier de vibrato. Lorsque c'est possible, la note à atteindre est indiquée.
a) Jouez le Sol et appuyez sur le levier de vibrato pour atteindre le Mi.
b) Jouez un Sol à vide et détendez le plus possible la corde avec le levier de vibrato pour rendre un effect de 'bombe qui tombe' (divebomb).

Hammer On et Pull Off
Jouez la première note; frappez la corde sur la touche (Hammer On) pour obtenir la seconde note, et relâchez la seconde note en tirant sur la corde (Pull Off) pour obtenir la troisième note. Seule la première note est donc jouée avec le médiator.

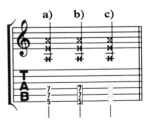

Mutes (étouffements)
a) Mute de la main droite
Etouffez en posant la main droite sur les cordes, au-dessus du chevalet.
b) Mute de la main gauche
Relâchez la pression sur la corde juste après avoir joué la note.
c) Mute sans hauteur définie
Etouffez les cordes avec la main gauche pour obtenir un son de percussion.

Glissando
a) Jouez la première note avec le médiator, faites sonner la seconde note en ne faisant que glisser le doigt sur la corde.
b) Comme ci-dessus, mais en attaquant également la seconde note avec le médiator.

Harmoniques naturelles
Posez le doigt sur la corde au dessus de la barrette indiquée, et jouez avec le médiator pour obtenir un son cristallin. Le cas échéant, une petite note indique la hauteur du son que l'on doit obtenir.

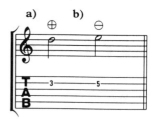

Guitare Slide
a) Note jouée avec le slide.
b) Note jouée sans le slide.

Harmoniques artificielles
Posez le doigt (main gauche) sur la note la plus basse: effleurez la corde avec l'index de la main droite au-dessus de la barrette indiquée par la note en forme de losange, tout en actionnant le médiator. La petite note indique la hauteur du son que l'on doit obtenir.

Effet de Vibrato
Jouez le vibrato soit avec le doigt sur la corde (main gauche), soit avec le levier de vibrato. Comme le vibrato est une affaire de technique et de goût personnels, il n'est indiqué que quand cela est vraiment nécessaire.

Harmoniques pincées
Appuyez le doigt sur la corde de la façon habituelle, mais utilisez conjointement le médiator et l'index de la main droite de façon á obtenir une harmonique aiguë. Les petites notes indiquent la hauteur du son que l'on doit obtenir.

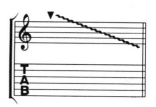

Scratch
Faites glisser le médiator du haut en bas de la corde. Le meilleur effet est obtenu avec des cordes filetées.

Quarts de ton
Une flèche dirigée vers le bas indique que la note est baissée d'un quart-de-ton. Une flèche dirigée vers le haut indique que la note est haussée d'un quart-de-ton.

Accords répétés
Pour faciliter la lecture des parties de guitare rythmique, les chiffres de tablature sont omis quand l'accord est répété. L'example montre successivement un accord de Do majeur joué de façon normale, un 'mute' de la main droite, un 'mute' de la main gauche et un 'mute' sans hauteur définie.

Accordages spéciaux
Les accordages non-standards sont indiqués par six cases, chacune représentant une corde (de gauche à droite), de la plus grave à la plus aiguë. Un tiret indique que la tension de la corde correspondante ne doit pas être altérée. Un nom de note indique la nouvelle note à obtenir. Pour les tablatures, les chiffres indiqués dans les cases représentent le nombre de demi-tons dont ou doit désaccorder la corde, vers le haut ou vers le bas.

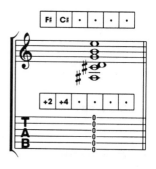

Accordez la corde de Mi grave un ton plus haut de façon à obtenir un Fa#, et la corde de La deux tons plus haut de façon à obtenir un Do#.

Noms des accords

Lorsqu'aucun nom d'accord précis n'est applicable, par exemple quand la musique consiste en une figure répétée (riff), le centre tonal est indiqué entre parenthèses: [C]

Lorsqu'un passage n'a pas pu être transcrit, le symbole ∿ apparait.

Hinweise zu Notation und Tabulatur

Offener C - Dur - Akkord

E - Dur - Tonleiter

— Hohe E-Saite (1.)
— H-Saite (2.)
— G-Saite (3.)
— D-Saite (4.)
— A-Saite (5.)
— Tiefe E-Saite (6.)

Gezogene Noten

Die gegriffene Note wird immer zuerst angegeben. Das Zeichen ⌐ ⌐ zeigt eine Veränderung der Tonhöhe an, die durch das Ziehen der Saiten erreicht wird. Falls Du nicht sicher bist, wie weit die Saite gezogen werden soll, spiele die entsprechenden Töne zunächst ohne Ziehen; so kannst Du Dich an der Tonhöhe orientieren. Die folgenden Beispiele geben die gebräuchlichsten Techniken zum Ziehen wieder:

Beispiel 1
Spiele das D und ziehe dann um einen Ton (zwei Halbtonschritte) höher zum E.

Beispiel 2
Spiele das D, ziehe um einen Ton hoch zum E und dann wieder zurück, so daß D erklingt. Dabei wird nur die erste Note angeschlagen.

Beispiel 3
Schnelles Ziehen: Spiele das D und ziehe dann so schnell Du kannst um einen Ton höher zum E.

Beispiel 4
Im Voraus gezogen: Greife das D, ziehe um einen Ton höher zum E und schlage erst dann die Saite an.

Beispiel 5
Spiele A und D gleichzeitig und ziehe dann die H-Saite um einen Ton nach oben, so daß H erklingt.

Beispiel 6
Spiele D und Fis gleichzeitig; ziehe dann die G-Saite um einen Ton nach oben zum E und die H-Saite um einen Halbtonschritt nach oben zum G.

Zusätzliche Spieltechniken für Gitarre wurden folgendermaßen notiert:

Tremolo
Verändere die Tonhöhe mit dem Tremolo-Hebel. Wenn es möglich ist, wird die angestrebte Tonhöhe angezeigt.
a) Spiele G; nutze den Takt, um zum E abzusteigen.
b) Spiele die leere G-Saite; nutze den Takt, um so weit wie möglich abzusteigen.

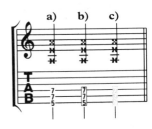

Dämpfen
a) Mit der rechten Hand
Dämpfe die Saiten, indem Du die rechte Hand einfach oberhalb der Brücke auf die Saiten legst.
b) Mit der linken Hand
Dämpfe die Saiten, indem Du den Druck der linken Hand löst, kurz nachdem die Töne erklingen.
c) Ohne bestimmte Tonhöhe
Dämpfe die Saiten mit der linken Hand; so erzielst Du einen 'geschlagenen' Sound.

Hammer on und Pull off
Spiele die erste Note; die zweite erklingt durch 'Hammering on', die dritte durch 'Pulling off'. Dabei wird nur die erste Note angeschlagen.

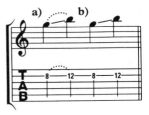

Glissando
a) Spiele die erste Note; die zweite erklingt durch Hochrutschen des Fingers auf der Saite. Nur die erste Note wird angeschlagen.
b) Wie oben, aber die zweite Note wird angeschlagen.

240

Natürliches Flageolett
Berühre die Saite über dem angegebenen Bund; wenn Du jetzt anschlägst, entsteht ein glockenähnlicher Ton. Wo es nötig ist, zeigen kleine Notenköpfe die entstandene Note an.

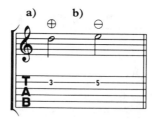

Slide Guitar
a) Spiele mit Rutschen des Fingers.
b) Spiele ohne Rutschen.

Künstliches Flageolett
Greife die unterste Note, berühre die Saite über dem durch Rauten angegebenen Bund und schlage dann den Ton an. Die kleinen Notenköpfe zeigen wieder die entstandene Note an.

Vibrato
Beim Vibrato läßt Du die Note für die Dauer eines Tons durch Druckvariation oder Tremolo-Hebel 'beben'. Da es jedoch eine Frage des persönlichen Geschmacks ist, wird Vibrato nur dort angegeben, wo es unerläßlich ist.

Gezupftes Flageolett
Greife die Note ganz normal, aber drücke die Saite mit der zupfenden Hand so, daß ein harmonischer Oberton entsteht. Kleine Notenköpfe zeigen den entstandenen Ton an.

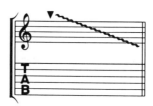

Pick Scratch
Fahre mit dem Plektrum nach unten über die Saiten – das klappt am besten bei umsponnenen Saiten.

Vierteltöne
Ein nach unten gerichteter Pfeil bedeutet, daß die notierte Tonhöhe um einen Viertelton erniedrigt wird; ein nach oben gerichteter Pfeil bedeutet, daß die notierte Tonhöhe um einen Viertelton erhöht wird.

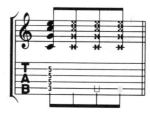

Akkordwiederholung
Um die Stimmen für Rhythmus-Gitarre leichter lesbar zu machen, werden die Tabulaturziffern weggelassen, wenn ein Akkord wiederholt werden soll. Unser Beispiel zeigt einen C - Dur - Akkord normal gespielt, rechts gedämpft, links gedämpft und ohne Tonhöhe.

Besondere Stimmung
Falls eine Stimmung verlangt wird, die vom Standard abweicht, wird sie in Kästchen angegeben. Jedes Kästchen steht für eine Saite, das erste links außen entspricht der tiefsten Saite. Wenn die Tonhöhe einer Saite nicht verändert werden soll, enthält das Kästchen einen Punkt. Steht eine Note im Kästchen, muß die Saite wie angegeben umgestimmt werden. In der Tabulaturschrift stehen stattdessen Ziffern im entsprechenden Kästchen: Sie geben die Zahl der Halbtonschritte an, um die eine Saite höher oder tiefer gestimmt werden soll.

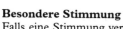
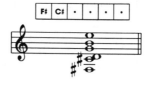

Stimme die tiefe E-Saite (6.) um einen Ganzton (zwei Halbtonschritte) höher auf Fis und die A-Saite (5.) um zwei Ganztöne (vier Halbtonschritte) höher auf Cis.

Akkordbezeichnung
Die folgenden Akkordbezeichnungen wurden verwendet.

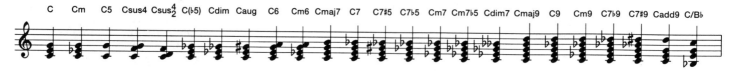

Wenn kein eigenes Akkordsymbol angegeben ist, z.B. bei Wiederholung einer musikalischen Figur (bzw. Riff), steht die Harmoniebezeichnung in Klammern: [C]

Das Symbol ~ steht jeweils dort, wo es nicht möglich war, einen Abschnitt zu übertragen.

Spiegazione della notazione e dell'intavolatura

Accordo di Do aperto
(in prima posizione)

Scala di Mi maggiore

Mi acuto: la corda
Si: 2a corda
Sol: 3a corda
Re: 4a corda
La: 5a corda
Mi basso: 6a corda

Bending

La prima nota scritta è sempre quella tastata normalmente. Le alterazioni di altezza da realizzare con la trazione laterale della corda (bending) interessano le note comprese sotto al segno: ⌐ ⌐. Se siete incerti sull'entità dell'innalzamento di tono da raggiungere, suonate le note indicate tastando normalmente la corda. Gli esempi seguenti mostrano le tecniche più comunemente impiegate nella maggior parte dei casi che possono presentarsi.

Esempio 1
Suonate il Re e innalzate di un tono (due mezzi toni) a Mi.

Esempio 2
Suonate il Re, tirate alzando di un tono a Mi e rilasciate tornando a Re. Va suonata solo la prima nota.

Esempio 3
'Bend Veloce': suonate il Re e quindi alzate di un tono a Mi il più velocemente possibile.

Esempio 4
'Pre-Bend': tastate il Re, tirate alzando di un tono a Mi e poi suonate.

Esempio 5
Suonate simultaneamente La e Si quindi tirate la 2a corda per innalzare il suono a Si.

Esempio 6
Suonate simultaneamente Re e Fa# quindi tirate la 3a corda alzando il suono di un tono a Mi, e la 2a corda di mezzo tono, alzando il suono a Sol.

Negli esempi seguenti sono illustrate altre tecniche chitarristiche:

Barra del tremolo
Alterate l'altezza del suono mediante la barra del tremolo. Dove possibile l'altezza da raggiungere è indicata.
a) Suonate il Sol e abbassate il suono fino a Mi mediante la barra.
b) Suonate il Sol a vuoto e scendete quanto più possibile.

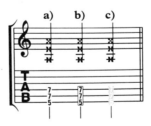

Smorzato
a) Smorzato con la destra
Smorzare le corde con il palmo della mano destra in prossimità del ponticello.
b) Smorzato con la sinistra
Smorzare le corde allentando la pressione delle dita subito dopo aver prodotto i suoni.
c) Pizzicato
Premere leggermente le corde in modo che non producano note ma soltanto un effetto percussivo.

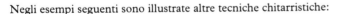

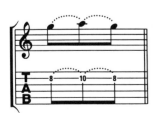

Legature ascendenti e discendenti
Suonate la prima nota e ricavate la seconda percuotendo la corda con il dito contro la barretta; per la terza nota tirate la corda con il medesimo dito. Soltano la prima nota va suonata.

Glissando
a) Suonate la prima nota e ricavare la seconda facendo scivolare il dito lungo la corda. Va pizzicata solo la prima nota.
b) Come sopra, ma pizzicando anche la seconda nota.

Armonici naturali

Toccate leggermente la corda sulla barretta indicata e pizzicate col plettro per produrre un suono di campana. Le notine indicano il suono risultante, dove occorra.

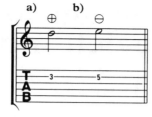

Slide Chitarra

a) Suonare con slide.
b) Suonare senza slide.

Armonici artificiali

Tastate la nota più bassa, toccate leggermente la corda sulla barretta relativa alla nota romboidale e pizzicate con il plettro. Le notine indicano il suono risultante.

Vibrato

Effettuate il vibrato facendo oscillare il dito che preme la corda oppure con la barra del tremolo. Poichè il vibrato è un fatto di gusto personale, viene indicato solo dove è essenziale.

Armonici pizzicati

Tastate normalmente la nota ma pizzicate la corda con la mano destra per ricavare l'armonico sopracuto. Le notine indicano l'altezza del suono risultante.

Suono graffiato

Fate scorrere il bordo del plettro lungo la corda. L'effetto è maggiore sulle corde fasciate.

Microintervalli

Una freccia diretta verso il basso significa che il suono scritto va abbassato di un intervallo inferiore al semitono; una freccia diretta verso l'alto innalza il suono scritto.

Accordi ripetuti

Per facilitare la lettura, possono venire omessi i numeri nell'intavolatura di un accordo ripetuto. L'esempio mostra un accordi di Do maggiore suonato normalmente, smorzato con la destra, smorzato con la sinistra e pizzicato (muto).

Accordature Speciali

Le accordature diverse da quella normale sono indicate in speciali 'gabbie di accordatura'. Ogni gabbia rappresenta una corda di chitarra; all'estremità sinistra corrisponde la corda più bassa. Il simbolo '•' in una gabbia sta ad indicare che l'intonazione della corda corrispondente è quella normale. Una nota nella gabbia indica che l'intonazione di quella corda va modificata portandola all'altezza indicata. Per coloro che leggono l'intavolatura, dei numeri posti nelle gabbie stanno ad indicare di quanti semitoni deve salire o scendere l'intonazione della corda. L'intavolatura è da considerarsi relativa ad uno strumento accordato come indicato nelle gabbie.

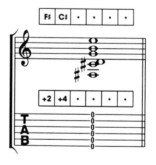

Accordate la corda del Mi basso (6a) un tono sopra (due semitoni) a Fa#.
Accordate la corda del La basso (5a) due toni sopra (quattro semitoni) a Do#.

Indicazione degli accordi

E' stata impiegata la seguente nomenclatura convenzionale degli accordi.

Quando non compare la griglia appropriata di un accordo, ad esempio, quando la musica consiste nella ripetizione di una stessa figura (riff), la base tonale è indicata fra parentesi: [C]

Dove non è stato possibile trascrivere il passaggio, compare il segno ~ .

Printed and bound in Great Britain